Breathe! You Are Alive

Breathe! You Are Alive

Sutra on the Full Awareness of Breathing

REVISED EDITION

THICH NHAT HANH

Parallax Press
Berkeley, California

Parallax Press
P.O. Box 7355
Berkeley, California 94707

Sutras translated from the Pali and Chinese by Thich Nhat Hanh,
    with Annabel Laity
Commentaries translated from the Vietnamese by Annabel Laity
Edited by Arnold Kotler
Cover drawing by Nguyen Thi Hop
Cover design by Gay Reineck
Text design by Legacy Media, Inc.

LIBRARY OF CONGRESS CATALOGING-IN-PUBLICATION DATA

Tipitaka. Suttapitaka. Majjhimanikaya. Anapanasatisutta. English &
Pali.
    Breathe! You are alive: sutra on the full awareness of breathing: with
commentary by Thich Nhat Hanh / translated from the Vietnamese by
Annabel Laity. Translation of: Anapanasatisutta.
    ISBN 0-938077-93-7
    I. Nhât Hanh, Thich. II. Laity, Annabel. III. Title.
BQ1320.A4822E5 1995.
294.3'823—dc19   88-15894

Contents

A NOTE ON THE TRANSLATION

The word for a Buddhist scripture, the teachings of the Buddha, is *sutta* in Pali and *sutra* in Sanskrit. This text, the *Anapanasati Sutta*, is of Pali origin, so it would be natural to use the Pali word "sutta" throughout the text. However, due to historical circumstance, Mahayana Sanskrit scriptures have become better known in the West, so we have decided to use the word "sutra" as if it were an English word. We use the word "sutta" only when it is part of the proper name of a Pali sutta, such as *Anapanasati Sutta* or *Satipatthana Sutta*. Otherwise, the word "sutra" is used to refer even to Pali texts. Secondly, there are no diacritical marks used in this translation because of the limitations of the publisher's software. Finally, we translate the term *sati* differently in the words *Anapanasati* and *Satipatthana*. In the former, we use "full awareness," and in the latter "mindfulness."

Breathe! You Are Alive

Breathe and you know that you are alive.
Breathe and you know that all is helping you.
Breathe and you know that you are the world.
Breathe and you know that the flower is breathing too.
Breathe for yourself and you breathe for the world.
Breathe in compassion and breathe out joy.

Breathe and be one with the air that you breathe.
Breathe and be one with the river that flows.
Breathe and be one with the earth that you tread.
Breathe and be one with the fire that glows.
Breathe and you break the thought of birth and death.
Breathe and you see that impermanence is life.

Breathe for your joy to be steady and calm.
Breathe for your sorrow to flow away.
Breathe to renew every cell in your blood.
Breathe to renew the depths of consciousness.
Breathe and you dwell in the here and now.
Breathe and all you touch is new and real.

—*Annabel Laity*

Sutra on the Full Awareness of Breathing

Sutra on the Full Awareness of Breathing

SECTION ONE

I heard these words of the Buddha one time when he was staying in Savatthi[1] in the Eastern Park, with many well-known and accomplished disciples, including Sariputta, Mahamoggallana, Mahakassapa, Mahakaccayana, Maha–kotthita, Mahakappina, Mahacunda, Anuruddha, Rewata, and Ananda. The senior *bhikkhus*[2] in the community were diligently instructing bhikkhus who were new to the practice—some instructing ten students, some twenty, some thirty, and some forty; and in this way the bhikkhus new to the practice gradually made great progress.

That night the moon was full, and the Pavarana Ceremony[3] was held to mark the end of the rainy-season retreat. Lord Buddha, the Awakened One, was sitting in the open air, and his disciples were gathered around him. After looking over the assembly, he began to speak:

"O bhikkhus, I am pleased to observe the fruit you have attained in your practice. Yet I know you can make even more progress. What you have not yet attained, you can attain. What you have not yet realized, you can realize perfectly. [To encourage your efforts,] I will stay here until the next full moon day."[4]

When they heard that the Lord Buddha was going to stay at Savatthi for another month, bhikkhus throughout the country began traveling there to study with him. The senior bhikkhus continued teaching the bhikkhus new to the practice even more ardently. Some were instructing ten bhikkhus, some twenty, some thirty, and some forty. With this help, the newer bhikkhus were able, little by little, to continue their progress in understanding.

When the next full moon day arrived, the Buddha, seated under the open sky, looked over the assembly of bhikkhus and began to speak:

"O bhikkhus, our community is pure and good. At its heart, it is without useless and boastful talk, and therefore it deserves to receive offerings and be considered a field of merit.[5] Such a community is rare, and any pilgrim who seeks it, no matter how far he must travel, will find it worthy.

"O bhikkhus, there are bhikkhus in this assembly who have realized the fruit of Arahatship,[6] destroyed every root of affliction,[7] laid aside every burden, and attained right understanding and emancipation. There are also bhikkhus who have cut off the first five internal formations[8] and realized the fruit of never returning to the cycle of birth and death.[9]

"There are those who have thrown off the first three internal formations and realized the fruit of returning once more.[10] They have cut off the roots of greed, hatred, and ignorance, and will only need to return to the cycle of birth and death one more time. There are those who have thrown off the three internal formations and attained the fruit of stream enterer,[11] coursing steadily to the Awakened State. There are those who practice the Four Establishments of Mindfulness.[12] There are those who practice the Four Right Efforts[13] and those who practice the Four Bases of Success.[14] There are those who practice the Five Faculties,[15] those who practice the Five Powers,[16] those who practice the Seven Factors of Awakening,[17] and those who practice the Noble Eightfold Path.[18] There are those who practice loving kindness, those who practice compassion, those who practice joy, and those who practice equanimity.[19] There are those who practice the Nine Contemplations,[20] and those who practice the Observation of Impermanence. There are also bhikkhus who are already practicing Full Awareness of Breathing."

SECTION TWO

"O bhikkhus, the method of being fully aware of breathing, if developed and practiced continuously, will have great rewards and bring great advantages. It will lead to success in practicing the Four Establishments of Mindfulness. If the method of the Four Establishments of Mindfulness is developed and practiced continuously, it will lead to success in the practice of the Seven Factors of Awakening. The Seven Factors of Awakening, if developed and practiced continuously, will give rise to understanding and liberation of the mind.

"What is the way to develop and practice continuously the method of Full Awareness of Breathing so that the practice will be rewarding and offer great benefit?

"It is like this, bhikkhus: the practitioner goes into the forest or to the foot of a tree, or to any deserted place, sits stably in the lotus position, holding his or her body quite straight, and practices like this: 'Breathing in, I know I am breathing in. Breathing out, I know I am breathing out.'

1. 'Breathing in a long breath, I know I am breathing in a long breath. Breathing out a long breath, I know I am breathing out a long breath.'

2. 'Breathing in a short breath, I know I am breathing in a short breath. Breathing out a short breath, I know I am breathing out a short breath.'

3. 'Breathing in, I am aware of my whole body. Breathing out, I am aware of my whole body.' He or she practices like this.

4. 'Breathing in, I calm my whole body. Breathing out, I calm my whole body.' He or she practices like this.

5. 'Breathing in, I feel joyful. Breathing out, I feel joy-ful.'²¹ He or she practices like this.

6. 'Breathing in, I feel happy. Breathing out, I feel happy.' He or she practices like this.

7. 'Breathing in, I am aware of my mental formations. Breathing out, I am aware of my mental formations.' He or she practices like this.

8. 'Breathing in, I calm my mental formations. Breathing out, I calm my mental formations.' He or she practices like this.

9. 'Breathing in, I am aware of my mind. Breathing out, I am aware of my mind.' He or she practices like this.

10. 'Breathing in, I make my mind happy. Breathing out, I make my mind happy.' He or she practices like this.

11. 'Breathing in, I concentrate my mind. Breathing out, I concentrate my mind.' He or she practices like this.

12. 'Breathing in, I liberate my mind. Breathing out, I liberate my mind.' He or she practices like this.

13. 'Breathing in, I observe the impermanent nature of all dharmas. Breathing out, I observe the impermanent nature of all dharmas.'²² He or she practices like this.

14. 'Breathing in, I observe the disappearance of desire. Breathing out, I observe the disappearance of desire.'[23] He or she practices like this.

15. 'Breathing in, I observe cessation. Breathing out, I observe cessation.'[24] He or she practices like this.

16. 'Breathing in, I observe letting go. Breathing out, I observe letting go.'[25] He or she practices like this.

"The Full Awareness of Breathing, if developed and practiced continuously according to these instructions, will be rewarding and of great benefit."

SECTION THREE

"In what way does one develop and continuously practice the Full Awareness of Breathing, in order to succeed in the practice of the Four Establishments of Mindfulness?

"When the practitioner breathes in or out a long or a short breath, aware of his breath or his whole body, or aware that he is making his whole body calm and at peace, he abides peacefully in the observation of the body in the body, persevering, fully awake, clearly understanding his state, gone beyond all attachment and aversion to this life. These exercises of breathing with Full Awareness belong to the first Establishment of Mindfulness, the body.

"When the practitioner breathes in or out aware of joy or happiness, of the mental formations, or to make the mental formations peaceful, he abides peacefully in the observation of the feelings in the feelings, persevering, fully awake, clearly understanding his state, gone beyond all attachment and aversion to this life. These exercises of breathing with Full Awareness belong to the second Establishment of Mindfulness, the feelings.

"When the practitioner breathes in or out with the awareness of the mind, or to make the mind happy, to collect the mind in concentration, or to free and liberate the mind, he abides peacefully in the observation of the mind in the mind, persevering, fully awake, clearly understanding his state, gone beyond all attachment and aversion to this life. These exercises of breathing with Full Awareness belong to the third Establishment of Mindfulness, the mind. Without Full Awareness of Breathing, there can be no development of meditative stability and understanding.

"When the practitioner breathes in or breathes out and contemplates the essential impermanence or the essential disappearance of desire or cessation or letting go, he abides peacefully in the observations of the objects of mind in the objects of mind, persevering, fully awake, clearly understanding his state, gone beyond all attachment and aversion to this life. These exercises of breathing with Full Awareness belong to the fourth Establishment of Mindfulness, the objects of mind.

"The practice of Full Awareness of Breathing, if developed and practiced continuously, will lead to perfect accomplishment of the Four Establishments of Mindfulness."

SECTION FOUR

"Moreover, if they are developed and continuously practiced, the Four Establishments of Mindfulness will lead to perfect abiding in the Seven Factors of Awakening. How is this so?

"When the practitioner can maintain, without distraction, the practice of observing the body in the body, the feelings in the feelings, the mind in the mind, and the objects of mind in the objects of mind, persevering, fully awake, clearly understanding his state, gone beyond all attachment and aversion to this life, with unwavering, steadfast, imperturbable meditative stability, he will attain the first Factor of Awakening, namely mindfulness. When this factor is developed, it will come to perfection.

"When the practitioner can abide in meditative stability without being distracted and can investigate every dharma, every object of mind that arises, then the second Factor of Awakening will be born and developed in him, the factor of investigating dharmas. When this factor is developed, it will come to perfection.

"When the practitioner can observe and investigate every dharma in a sustained, persevering, and steadfast way, without being distracted, the third Factor of Awakening will be born and developed in him, the factor of energy. When this factor is developed, it will come to perfection.

"When the practitioner has reached a stable, imperturbable abiding in the stream of practice, the fourth Factor of Awakening will be born and developed in him, the factor of joy.[26] When this factor is developed, it will come to perfection.

"When the practitioner can abide undistractedly in the state of joy, he will feel his body and mind light and at peace. At this point the fifth Factor of Awakening will be born and developed, the factor of ease. When this factor is developed, it will come to perfection.

"When both body and mind are at ease, the practitioner can easily enter into concentration. At this point the sixth Factor of Awakening will be born and developed in him, the factor of concentration. When this factor is developed, it will come to perfection.

"When the practitioner is abiding in concentration with deep calm, he will cease discriminating and comparing.[27] At this point the seventh factor of Awakening is released, born, and developed in him, the factor of letting go.[28] When this factor is developed, it will come to perfection.

"This is how the Four Establishments of Mindfulness, if developed and practiced continuously, will lead to perfect abiding in the Seven Factors of Awakening."

SECTION FIVE

"How will the Seven Factors of Awakening, if developed and practiced continuously, lead to the perfect accomplishment of true understanding and complete liberation?

"If the practitioner follows the path of the Seven Factors of Awakening, living in quiet seclusion, observing and contemplating the disappearance of desire, he will develop the capacity of letting go. This will be a result of following the path of the Seven Factors of Awakening and will lead to the perfect accomplishment of true understanding and complete liberation."

SECTION SIX

This is what the Lord, the Awakened One, said; and everyone in the assembly felt gratitude and delight at having heard his teachings.

—Majjhima Nikaya, Sutta No. 118, translated from the Pali

Commentaries on the Sutra

CHAPTER ONE
A Brief History

The *Sutra on the Full Awareness of Breathing* presented here
is a translation from the Pali of the *Anapanasati Sutta*.[29] In
the Chinese Tripitaka, there is a *Da An Ban Shou Yi Jing*
(*Greater Anapanasati Sutta*).[30]

This text cites An Shi Gao as translator into Chinese. Master Shi Gao was a Parthian[31] by birth who went to China in
the later Han period. There is also a preface to this sutra
written by Master Tang Hôi. The *Da An Ban Shou Yi Jing*
seems to be different from the Pali *Anapanasati* and is probably a commentary on it and not just an expansion or em-
bellishment of it. At the end of the text, the engraver of the
wood block says, "Judging from the style of the sutra, it
seems the copyist is at fault: the original text and the commentary are so intertwined that it is no longer possible to
distinguish between them."

The original translation by Shi Gao of the Sanskrit (or
Prakrit) text into Chinese has probably been lost. The *Da An
Ban Shou Yi Jing* is only the commentary that was originally
printed below the text of the sutra. It does not begin with the
words that usually begin a sutra, "Thus have I heard." According to Tang Hôi's preface, the person responsible for the
annotation and commentary was Chen Hui, and Tang Hôi
himself only assisted in the work by correcting, altering, and
editing it.

Chen Hui was a disciple of Master An Shi Gao, who travelled from Loyang, China, to Giao Chi (present-day Tonkin or North Vietnam) with two fellow disciples, Gan Lin and Pi Ye. They may have brought the original translation of the *Anapanasati Sutta* with them. The commentary and preface were written by Tang Hôi in Vietnam before the year 229 C.E.

Tang Hôi's parents were traders from Sogdia in central Asia who had settled in Vietnam, and Tang Hôi was born in Vietnam, became a monk in Vietnam, and studied Sanskrit and Chinese there. Before traveling to the kingdom of Wu in southern China in the year 255 to spread the Dharma, he had already taught the Dharma in Vietnam and had already composed and translated many works into Chinese. He died in the kingdom of Wu in the year 280.

In the Chinese *Tripitaka*, there are a number of other sutras on the Full Awareness of Breathing: *Zeng Yi A Han*, *Ekottara Agama*, chapters seven and eight on the theme "Awareness of Breathing,"[32] the sutra *Xiu Hang Dao Di*, Book Five, chapter twenty-three, on "Breath Counting,"[33] and in the *Tsa A Han* (*Samyukta Agama* sutra collection), the chapter on Full Awareness of Breathing.[34] If we combine the three sutras 815, 803 and 810 of this collection, we have the equivalent of the Pali *Anapanasati*. A translation of these three sutras from the Chinese can be found at the end of this book.

The sutra already presented here in English is a translation from the original *Anapanasati Sutta* in the Pali *Tipitaka* (Sanskrit: *Tripitaka*). In many countries of the Mahayana tradition, the *Anapanasati Sutta (Full Awareness of Breathing)* and the *Satipatthana Sutta (Four Establishments of*

Mindfulness)[35] are not considered important and, in some cases, are not even available for study. There are Buddhist centers where practitioners are considered to have learned all there is to know about the Four Establishments of Mindfulness when they can repeat that the body is impure, the feelings are painful, the mind is impermanent, and the objects of mind are without self. There is even one book on Buddhist meditation that says that the practice of meditation does not need Mindfulness of Breathing or the Four Establishments of Mindfulness. The Four Establishments of Mindfulness are a daily practice, described in great detail in the *Anapanasati* and *Satipatthana Suttas*. These two texts, along with the *Bhaddekaratta Sutta* (*Sutra on Knowing the Better Way to Live Alone*),[36] are fundamental to the practice of meditation, and the author of this commentary feels that it is very important to reestablish the importance of these three texts in all places of study and meditation.

In the Southern traditions of Buddhism, the *Full Awareness of Breathing* and the *Four Establishments of Mindfulness* are still regarded as the most important texts on meditation. Many monks learn these sutras by heart and give them their greatest attention. Even though the spirit of these sutras is very much present and observable in the Mahayana meditation sutras, we would do well to become familiar with the sutra literature fundamental to meditation that was studied and practiced at the time of the Buddha. The author hopes that these texts will again be put into wide circulation in the Northern traditions of Buddhism. If we understand the essence of these two sutras, we will have a deeper vision and more comprehensive grasp of the scriptures classified as

Mahayana, just as after we see the roots and the trunk of a tree, we can appreciate its leaves and branches more deeply.

From these sutras, we observe that practitioners of meditation at the time of the Buddha did not consider the Four *Jhanas*,[37] the Four Formless Concentrations,[38] and the Nine Concentration Attainments to be essential to the practice. The Four Jhanas are mental states in which the practitioner abandons the desire realm and enters the realm of form, and although his or her mind remains perfectly awake, the five sense perceptions no longer arise. These four successive states (also called Four Absorptions) are followed by the Four Formless Concentrations, which are states of meditation in which the practitioner, having already abandoned the realms of form, enters four successive formless realms: (1) The Realm of Limitless Space, (2) The Realm of Limitless Consciousness, (3) The Realm Where Nothing Exists, and (4) The Realm Where the Concepts "Perceiving" and "Not Perceiving" No Longer Apply. The Nine Concentration Attainments are composed of the Four Jhanas and the Four Formless Concentrations, plus the attainment of cessation (*nirodha samapatti*), a concentration in which there is the absence of feeling and perception. There are many references in other sutras of the Southern traditions as well as in those of the Northern traditions to the Four Jhanas, the Four Formless Concentrations and the Nine Concentration Attainments, but in these two basic sutras (*Full Awareness of Breathing* and *Four Establishments of Mindfulness*), there are no such references. Thus we can infer that the Four Jhanas, the Four Formless Concentrations, and the Nine Concentration Attainments became a part of Buddhist practice after the death of the Buddha, probably due to the influence of the Vedic and other Yogic meditation schools outside of Buddhism. The teachers who introduced them gave them a Buddhist flavor and adapted them so they would fit with a Buddhist way of practice.

In the oldest Buddhist scriptures: the *Dhammapada*, the *Suttanipata*, the *Theragatha*, the *Therigatha*, the *Itivuttaka*, and the *Udana*, as well as in some of the most important other sutras: *The Turning of the Dharma Wheel*, the *Anapanasati*, and the *Satipatthana*, there is no mention of the Four Jhanas. But because they are mentioned in so many other suttas we generally think they were a method of practice taught by the Buddha. However, from my research, it seems to me that the Four Jhanas, the Four Formless Concentrations, and the Nine Concentration Attainments were not introduced into Buddhism as Buddhist practices until one hundred years after the Buddha's passing. When we read the life story of the Buddha in the sutras, in the *Vinaya*, and in the account by Asvagosa, we learn that before the Buddha was enlightened, he practiced meditation under the guidance of two teachers, Arada Kalama and Udraka Ramaputra. He practiced the Four Formless Concentrations with great success, but he expressed clearly that this practice did not lead to final liberation from suffering, and therefore he abandoned it. One of the reasons the Nine Concentration Attainments were made a part of Buddhist practice might have been that people feel the need for a practice marked by stages of progress, and here there is a progression from the first jhana, through the Four Formless Concentrations, to the cessation attainment.

Therefore, we may conclude that according to the *Anapanasati* and *Satipatthana Suttas*, the realization of the Four

Jhanas and the Four Formless Concentrations is dispensable. Future generations of scholars should distinguish as much as possible between the essential, fundamental meditation practices of Buddhism (whether Northern or Southern), and elements that were incorporated later from other traditions. Throughout the history of Buddhism, new elements have always been added. This is the only way Buddhism can grow and stay alive. In the eighth century and afterwards, *kung an* (*koan*) practice developed. Some new methods have been very successful, and some have failed. Before we study and practice methods of meditation practice that were developed after the time of the Buddha, we should first firmly grasp the ways of meditation that the Buddha taught and practiced with his disciples after his enlightenment.

Analyzing their content, we can see that the *Anapanasati* and *Satipatthana Suttas* are perfectly compatible with one another. Throughout 2,600 years of Buddhist history, all generations of the Buddha's disciples have respected these works and have not embellished them (as they have so many other scriptures). Although the *Anapanasati Sutta* was in circulation in Vietnam as early as the beginning of the third century C.E., from the time Vietnamese Buddhists devoted themselves primarily to the study of great and beautiful Mahayana sutras like the *Avatamsaka*, the *Lotus*, and the *Vimalakirti Nirdesa*, this sutra ceased to be regarded as essential. It is time for us to restore the *Sutra on the Full Awareness of Breathing* to its proper place in the tradition of meditation practice. We can begin to practice mindfulness of breathing as soon as we enter a Buddhist meditation center.

CHAPTER TWO

Summary of the Content

The sixteen methods of inhaling and exhaling, in combination with the Four Establishments of Mindfulness, are the essence of the *Sutra on the Full Awareness of Breathing.* Breathing is a means of awakening and maintaining full attention in order to look carefully, long, and deeply, see the nature of all things, and arrive at liberation.

Everything that exists can be placed into one of the Four Establishments of Mindfulness—namely the body, the feelings, the mind, and the objects of the mind. "All dharmas" is another way of saying "the objects of the mind." Although all dharmas are divided into four, in reality they are one, because all Four Establishments of Mindfulness are all objects of the mind.

The sixteen methods of breathing in and breathing out presented in this sutra can be divided into four groups of four methods each. The first group uses the body as the object of Full Awareness; the second uses the feelings; the third, the mind; and the fourth, the objects of mind.

After explaining the sixteen methods of conscious breathing, the Buddha speaks about the Four Establishments of Mindfulness and the Seven Factors of Awakening. He then reminds us that if the methods of fully aware breathing are practiced continuously, they will lead to the realization of the Seven Factors of Awakening. The Buddha speaks in greater detail about the Four Establishments of Mindfulness in the *Satipatthana Sutta*. The Seven Factors of Awakening are also discussed again in the *Satipatthana Sutta* and in other sutras. The main point of this sutra is the practice of Full Awareness of Breathing combined with the practice of the Four Establishments of Mindfulness.

CHAPTER THREE

Analysis of the Sutra's Content

The Sutra on the Full Awareness of Breathing can be divided into six sections:

SECTION ONE
THE SCENE

The first part of the sutra describes the circumstances under which the Buddha delivered this Dharma talk. We are told about the community of his disciples during the time he was staying at the Eastern Park, a large park with many trees located right outside the city of Savatthi. The number of monks staying with the Buddha at that time may have been more than four hundred. The senior monks each taught ten, twenty, thirty or forty newer monks.

Every morning after sitting in meditation, the monks went into the city together, bowls in hand, to beg for food. Before midday, when the sun was directly overhead, they returned to their retreat center to eat. From time to time, they would all be invited to eat at the king's palace or at the home of a wealthy patron, someone whose home was large enough to accommodate so many monks. Poorer households would wait for the bhikkhus to walk by, so they too could make offerings. There were also some people who would bring food to the park to offer to the community.

The Buddha and his disciples ate only one meal a day, before noon. There was no cooking or baking at the retreat center itself. The monks had no responsibility for performing funerals or praying for sick or deceased laypersons, as is the case today in many Buddhist countries. Instead they offered a brief lecture to their sponsors either before or after eating the meal offered by them. They were able to speak clearly and powerfully, because they were living an integrated life, putting their study into practice.

While the sun was still up, the Buddha would teach his disciples under a shady grove of trees. Sometimes, he would also give a Dharma talk in the evening, if the moon was bright enough, as is the case with this sutra. The Buddha had previously explained aspects of the practice of the Full Awareness of Breathing a number of times (there were many disciples already practicing it), but the evening he delivered this sutra was probably the first time he taught the entire method completely. He probably chose this occasion because there were so many bhikkhus from all over the country present, including a number of new disciples.

That year the retreat of the Buddha and his disciples in the Eastern Park was extended an additional month, to four months, so there would be a chance for disciples from all over the country to be together in one place. Many monks were able to be there because they had completed their rainy-season retreats one month earlier than the monks staying at the Eastern Park. There may have been as many as one thousand bhikkhus present the evening the Lord Buddha delivered the *Sutra on the Full Awareness of Breathing.*

SECTION TWO
THE SIXTEEN EXERCISES

The second section is the heart of the sutra. This section elaborates the sixteen methods of fully aware breathing in connection with the Four Establishments of Mindfulness.

THE FOUR PRELIMINARY EXERCISES

"Breathing in, I know I am breathing in. Breathing out, I know I am breathing out."

1. "Breathing in a long breath, I know I am breathing in a long breath. Breathing out a long breath, I know I am breathing out a long breath."

2. "Breathing in a short breath, I know I am breathing in a short breath. Breathing out a short breath, I know I am breathing out a short breath."

3. "Breathing in, I am aware of my whole body. Breathing out, I am aware of my whole body."

4. "Breathing in, I calm my whole body. Breathing out, I calm my whole body."

The first four exercises of fully aware breathing help us return to our body in order to look deeply at it and care for it. In our daily lives, it is important that we learn to create harmony and ease in our body, and to reunite body and mind. The Buddha never taught us to mistreat or oppress our bodies.

In exercises one and two, the object of awareness is our breath itself. Our mind is the subject, and our breathing is the object. Our breath may be short, long, heavy, or light. Practicing awareness in this way, we see that our breathing affects our mind, and our mind affects our breathing. Our mind and our breath become one. We also see that breathing is an aspect of the body and that awareness of breathing is also awareness of the body.

In the third exercise, the breath is connected with our whole body, not just a part of it. Awareness of the breathing is, at the same time, awareness of our entire body. Our mind, our breath, and our whole body are one.

In the fourth breathing exercise, our body's functions begin to calm down. Calming the breath is accompanied by calming the body and the mind. Our mind, our breathing, and our body are calmed down, equally.

In these four breathing exercises, we can realize the oneness of body and mind. Breathing is an excellent tool for establishing calmness and evenness.

THE SECOND FOUR EXERCISES

5. *"Breathing in, I feel joyful. Breathing out, I feel joyful."*
6. *"Breathing in, I feel happy. Breathing out, I feel happy."*
7. *"Breathing in, I am aware of my mental formations. Breathing out, I am aware of my mental formations."*
8. *"Breathing in, I calm my mental formations. Breathing out, I calm my mental formations."*

The second four exercises of fully aware breathing help us return to our feelings in order to develop joy and happiness and transform suffering. Our feelings are us. If we do not look after them, who will do it for us? Every day, we have painful feelings, and we need to learn how to look after them. Our teachers and friends can help us to a certain extent, but we have to do the work. Our body and our feelings are our territory, and we are the king responsible for that territory.

Practicing the fifth exercise, we touch pleasant, unpleasant, and neutral feelings. As a result of conscious breathing and calming the body (*kayasamskara*, the fourth method), joy, a pleasant feeling, arises.

In the sixth exercise, joy is transformed into peace and happiness, and we are fully aware of it. The seventh and eighth exercises bring our attention to all feelings that arise, whether produced by the body or the mind (*cittasamskara*). The mind's functions include feelings and perceptions. When we are aware of every bodily and every mental action, we are aware of every feeling.

The eighth exercise calms the body and mind and makes them peaceful. At this point, we can perfectly and completely unify body, mind, feelings, and breath.

THE NEXT FOUR EXERCISES

9. "Breathing in, I am aware of my mind. Breathing out, I am aware of my mind."

10. "Breathing in, I make my mind happy. Breathing out, I make my mind happy."

11. "Breathing in, I concentrate my mind. Breathing out, I concentrate my mind."

12. "Breathing in, I liberate my mind. Breathing out, I liberate my mind."

The third four exercises of fully aware breathing have to do with our mind, which means the activities of our mind. Buddhist psychology in the Vijñanavada tradition lists fifty-one mental functions (cittasamskara). These exercises help

us deal with whatever mental formations are present, culti-
vating mental formations that are beneficial, and being in
touch with and transforming mental formations that are not
beneficial. Mental formations are part of our territory, also.
There are seeds buried deep in our consciousness that we do
not touch often enough, seeds of love, understanding, compassion, joy, knowing right from wrong, the ability to listen
to others, nonviolence, and the willingness to overcome ignorance, aversion, and attachment. Through the practice of
mindfulness, we learn to identify these traits in us and nur-
ture them, with the help of teachers and spiritual friends,
until they grow into beautiful flowers. When we survey our
territory, we also find destructive traits, such as anger, de-
spair, suspicion, pride, and other mental formations that
cause us suffering. Because we do not like to look at these
negative traits, we do not want to come back to ourselves.
But with the aid of the practice of mindful breathing, we
learn to take full responsibility for restoring our territory
and taking good care of it.

The tenth exercise makes our mind happy, because it is
easier for the mind to become concentrated when it is in a
peaceful, happy state than when it is filled with sorrow or
anxiety. We are aware that we have the opportunity to practice meditation and that there is no moment as important
as the present one. Calmly abiding in the present moment,
immense joy arises each time we touch in ourselves the seeds
of faith, compassion, goodness, equanimity, liberty, and so
on. These seeds are buried deep in our consciousness, and
we need only to touch them and water them with conscious
breathing for them to manifest.

Using the mind to observe the mind, the eleventh exercise brings us to deep concentration. Mind is the breath. Mind is the oneness of the subject that illumines and the object that is illuminated. Mind is peace and happiness. Mind is the field of illumination and the strength of concentration. All mental formations that manifest in the present moment can become objects of our concentration.

The twelfth exercise can release the mind to freedom, if it is still bound. Mind is bound either because of the past or the future, or because of other latent desires or anger. With clear observation, we can locate the knots that are binding us, making it impossible for our mind to be free and at peace. We loosen these knots and untie the ropes that bind our mind. Full Awareness of Breathing shines into the mind the light of the observation that can illumine and set the mind free. Looking deeply at the nature of mental formations such as fear, anger, anxiety, and so on brings about the understanding that will liberate us.

THE FOUR FINAL EXERCISES

13. "*Breathing in, I observe the impermanent nature of all dharmas. Breathing out, I observe the impermanent nature of all dharmas.*"

14. "*Breathing in, I observe the disappearance of desire. Breathing out, I observe the disappearance of desire.*"

15. "*Breathing in, I observe cessation. Breathing out, I observe cessation.*"

16. "*Breathing in, I observe letting go. Breathing out, I observe letting go.*"

Mind cannot be separated from its object. Mind is consciousness, feeling, attachment, aversion, and so on. Consciousness must always be conscious of something. Feeling
is always feeling something. Loving and hating are always
loving and hating something. This "something" is the object
of the mind. Mind cannot arise if there is no object. Mind
cannot exist if the object of mind does not exist. The mind
is, at one and the same time, the subject of consciousness and the object of consciousness. All physiological phenomena, such as the breath, the nervous system, and the
sense organs; all psychological phenomena, such as feelings,
thoughts, and consciousness; and all physical phenomena,
such as the earth, water, grass, trees, mountains, and rivers,
are objects of mind, and therefore all are mind. All of them
can be called "dharmas."

The thirteenth breathing exercise sheds light on the ever-
changing, impermanent nature of all that exists—the psychological, the physiological, and the physical. Breathing
itself is also impermanent. The insight into impermanence
is very important, because it opens the way for us to see the
interrelated, inter-conditioned nature as well as the selfless
nature (nothing has a separate, independent self) of all that
exists.

The fourteenth exercise allows us to recognize the true
nature of our desire, to see that every dharma is already in
the process of disintegrating, so that we are no longer pos-
sessed by the idea of holding onto any dharma as an object
of desire and as a separate entity, even the physiological and
psychological elements in ourselves.

The fifteenth exercise allows us to arrive at the awareness
of a great joy, the joy of emancipation and the cessation of

illusion, by freeing us from the intention to grasp any notion.

The sixteenth exercise illuminates for us what it is to let go of ourselves, to give up all the burdens of our ignorance and our grasping. To be able to let go is already to have arrived at liberation.

These sixteen exercises can be studied and practiced intelligently. Although the first four preliminary exercises help our concentration very much, and every time we practice it is helpful to do these, it is not always necessary to practice the sixteen exercises in sequence. For example, you might like to practice only the fourteenth exercise for several days or months.

Although these exercises are presented very simply, their effectiveness is immeasurable. Depending on our experience, we can enter them deeply or superficially. The Lord Buddha did not intend to generate new theories or to confuse the minds of those new to the practice, so he used simple terms, like impermanence, disappearance of desire, cessation, and letting go. In fact, the deeper meaning of the term impermanence also includes the concepts of non-self, emptiness, interbeing, signlessness (*alaksana*), and aimlessness (*apranihita*). That is why it is so important to observe deeply that which lights our path and leads to emancipation.

SECTION THREE
THE FOUR ESTABLISHMENTS OF MINDFULNESS

The third part of the sutra is concerned with the Four Establishments of Mindfulness. These are referred to in the second section, although not by name. In this sutra, the Four Establishments are only briefly expounded. We must read the *Satipatthana Sutta* to study the subject in more detail.[39] The Four Establishments are the body, the feelings, the mind, and all *dharmas* (objects of mind). In this sutra, we practice full awareness of the Four Establishments through conscious breathing.

I want to say something about the phrases "observing the body in the body," "observing the feelings in the feelings," "observing the mind in the mind," and "observing the objects of mind in the objects of mind," which appear in the third section of the sutra. The key to "observation meditation" is that the subject of observation and the object of observation not be regarded as separate. A scientist might try to separate herself from the object she is observing and measuring, but students of meditation have to remove the boundary between subject and object. When we observe something, we *are* that thing. "Non-duality" is the key word. "Observing the body in the body" means that in the process of observing, we do not stand outside our own body as if we are an independent observer, but we identify ourselves one hundred percent with the object being observed. This is the only path that can lead us to the penetration and direct experience of reality. In "observation meditation," the body and mind are one entity, and the subject and object of meditation are one entity also. There is no sword of discrimination that slices reality into many parts. The meditator is a fully engaged participant, not a separate observer.

"Observation meditation" is a lucid awareness of what is going on in the Four Establishments: body, feelings, mind, and all dharmas, "persevering, fully awake, clearly understanding his state, gone beyond all attachment and aversion to this life." "Life" means all that exists. Stubbornly clinging to all that exists or resisting and rejecting it all both lack the lucidity of an awakened mind. To succeed in the work of observation, we must go beyond both attachment and aversion.

SECTION FOUR
THE SEVEN FACTORS OF AWAKENING

In the fourth section of the sutra, the Buddha discusses the arising, growth, and attainment of the Seven Factors of Awakening, through abiding in them in conjunction with conscious breathing.

(1) Full attention is the main Factor of Awakening. Full attention is awareness, being fully awake. If full attention is developed and maintained, the practice of observation to shed light on and see clearly all that exists will meet with success. (2) The work of observation to shed light on the object of our attention and see clearly all that exists is investigation of dharmas. (3) Energy is perseverance and diligence. (4-5) Joy and ease are wonderful feelings nourished by energy. (6) Concentration gives rise to understanding. When we have understanding, we can go beyond all comparing, measuring, discriminating, and reacting with attachment and aversion. (7) Going beyond is letting go. Those who arrive at letting go will have the bud of a half-smile, which proves compassion as well as understanding.

SECTION FIVE
EMANCIPATION

In the fifth section, which is very short, the Buddha reminds us that the Seven Factors of Awakening, if practiced diligently, lead to true understanding and emancipation.

SECTION SIX
CONCLUSION

The sixth section is the concluding sentence of the sutra. This sentence is used at the end of every sutra.

CHAPTER FOUR

A Point of View on the Practice

Neither the *Sutra on the Full Awareness of Breathing* nor the *Sutra on the Four Establishments of Mindfulness* mentions the technique of counting the breath. There is also no mention of the Six Wonderful Dharma Doors: counting, following, stopping, observing, returning, and calming. Nor is there any reference to the *kasina* (visualized image) meditation, the Four Jhanas, or the Four Formless Concentrations. These teachings were probably developed somewhat later to serve many levels of students. We need not criticize them for being later teachings, certainly not before we have practiced them and seen for ourselves if they work well.

Counting is an excellent technique for beginners.[40] Breathing in, count "one." Breathing out, count "one." Breathing in, count "two." Breathing out, count "two." Continue up to ten and then start counting over again. If at any time you forget where you are, begin again with "one." The method of counting helps us refrain from dwelling on troublesome thoughts; instead we concentrate on our breathing and the number. When we have developed some control over our thinking, counting may become tedious and we can abandon it and just follow the breath itself. This is called "following."

Well-known commentaries, such as the *Patisambhida Magga* (*Path of No Hesitation*) and the *Visuddhi Magga* (*Path of Purity*), teach that while we breathe, we should be aware of our nostrils, the place where air enters and leaves the body. Just as when we cut a log we keep our eyes on the place where the saw touches the log (rather than looking at the teeth of the saw), we pay attention to the nostrils and not to the air as it enters the body. Many commentators point out that if you follow the breath entering the body, then the object of your attention is not a single object, and thus concentration will be difficult. For this reason, they say that "the whole body" in the third method means the whole body of breath and not the whole body of the practitioner. If we study the sutra, we can see that their explanation is not correct. In the third breathing exercise, the object of attention is not just the breath. It *is* the whole body of the practitioner, in the same way that the object of the seventh exercise is all feelings and the object of the ninth exercise is the whole mind.

In the fourth exercise (*"Breathing in, I calm my whole body"*), the expression "whole body" cannot mean just the whole body of breath either. All four preliminary exercises take the physical body as the object, since the body is the first of the Four Establishments of Mindfulness. Even if in the first two exercises the object is just the breathing, that includes the body, since the breath is a part of our physical organism. In the third and fourth exercises, the entire physical body is the object.

All the commentaries—the *Patisambhida Magga* (*Path of No Hesitation*) by Mahanama, the *Vimutti Magga* (*Path of Liberation*) by Upatissa, and the *Visuddhi Magga* (*Path of Purity*) by Buddhaghosa—recommend that practitioners focus on the tip of the nose rather than follow the breath as it enters the body. If the practitioner follows the breath into the body, they say, the practitioner will be dispersed and unable to enter into the Four Jhanas. The *Vimutti Magga* was written at the end of the fourth century C.E., the *Patisambhida Magga* at the beginning of the fifth, and the *Visuddhi Magga* shortly after that. All of these emphasize the necessity of stopping (*samatha*) as the prerequisite for observing (*vipasyana*). Here, stopping means the Four Jhanas and the Four Formless Concentrations. Focusing the mind at the tip of the nose and being aware of the first moment of contact of air at its place of entry into the body, just as the carpenter looks only at the place of contact of the saw's teeth as they enter and leave the wood, gradually the rough, uneven breathing becomes delicate and subtle, and finally all discrimination disappears. At this point, the sign (kasina) will appear, like a ball of cotton, giving the practitioner a feeling of lightness and ease like a fresh, cool breeze. If the practitioner follows this sign, he or she enters concentration, the first of the Four Jhanas. The first jhana is the first step, followed by the second, third, and fourth jhanas. In each state of meditative concentration, the five sense organs are inactive, while the mind of the practitioner is lucid and awake. After the Four Jhanas come the Four Formless Concentrations: the realm of limitless space, the realm of limitless consciousness, the realm of no materiality, and the realm where the concepts "perceiving" and "not perceiving" no longer apply.

We must examine the extent to which Buddhist meditation practice was influenced by the Yoga-Upanishadic systems. Before realizing the Way, Shakyamuni Buddha studied with many Brahman yogis, from whom he learned the Four Jhanas and the Four Formless Concentrations. After experiencing these, he said that concentrations like "the realm of no materiality" and "the realm where perceiving and not perceiving do not apply," taught by the masters Arada Kalama and Udraka Ramaputra, cannot lead to ultimate emancipation. As we have seen, he did not mention the Four Jhanas or the Four Formless Concentrations in the *Anapanasati* or the *Satipatthana*, the two fundamental sutras on meditation. Therefore, we must conclude that the practices of the Four Jhanas and the Four Formless Concentrations are not necessary for arriving at the fruit of practice, the awakened mind. The methods of mindfulness taught by the Buddha in the *Sutra on the Four Establishments of Mindfulness* can be seen as the incomparable path leading to emancipation. There are meditation students who have practiced for many years and who, having failed to attain the Four Jhanas, think they do not have the capacity to realize awakening. There are others who stray into unhealthy meditation practices and lose all peace of mind, just because they want so much to enter the Four Jhanas. Only by practicing correctly, according to the teachings of the Buddha in the *Anapanasati* and *Satipatthana Suttas*, can we be sure we will not stray into practices we may later regret.

In Vietnam, the home country of the author, at the beginning of the third century C.E., the meditation master Tang Hôi, when writing the preface to the *Anapanasati* in Chinese, referred to the Four Jhanas, but the Four Jhanas of Tang Hôi were combined with observation—observing the body, sky and earth, prosperity and decline, coming and going, and so on. Tang Hôi also spoke of the Six Wonderful Dharma Doors (counting the breath, following the breath, concentrating the mind, observing to throw light on all that exists, returning to the source of mind, and going beyond the concepts of subject and object). Moreover, Tang Hôi referred to the technique of concentrating the mind at the tip of the nose. The *Xiu Hang Dao Di Sutra*, in the chapter called "Enumerating,"[41] also refers to the Four Jhanas, the technique of counting the breath, the Six Wonderful Dharma Doors, and the technique of concentrating the mind at the tip of the nose. The *Zeng Yi A Han (Ekottara Agama)*,[42] in the chapter on breathing, also refers to the Four Jhanas and the technique of concentrating the mind at the tip of the nose, but it does not refer to counting the breath or the Six Wonderful Dharma Doors.

We should remember that the sutras were memorized and transmitted orally for hundreds of years before they were written down. Therefore, many sutras must have been at least somewhat altered according to a variety of influences and circumstances during those centuries. The *Anapanasati* and *Satipatthana Suttas* can be seen as two precious accounts of early Buddhist meditation practice since they were handed down by the monks in an especially careful way. It seems to be the case that mistakes and outside additions were very few in these two sutras.

In the history of Buddhism, some classical sutras were affected during their transmission by outside influences, both in the Southern schools and the Northern schools, but especially in the Northern schools. Studying Mahayana sutras, we must remember to look again and discover the depth of the fundamental "source" sutras. The seeds of all important ideas of the Mahayana are already contained in these "source" sutras. If we go back to the "source," we develop a more clear and unshakable view of the Mahayana sutras. If we merely sit on the two giant wings of the Mahayana bird, we may fly far away and lose all contact with the original abode from which the bird arose.

Although the *Anapanasati* and *Satipatthana Suttas* do not refer to the Four Jhanas and the Four Formless Concentrations, we should not conclude that they do not emphasize the importance of concentration. Meditation has two aspects: stopping (samatha), and observation or looking deeply (vipasyana). Stopping is concentration, and looking deeply is insight. The Full Awareness of the Breath, or of any other object such as the body, the feelings, the mind, the objects of mind, and so forth, all aim at the goal of concentrating the mind on an object so that it is possible to see the object in all its depth. Concentrating the mind is stopping it from running around from one object to another in order to stay with just one object. We stay with one object in order to observe it and look deeply into it. In this way, stopping and observing become one.

Thanks to our ability to stop, we are able to observe. The more deeply we observe, the greater our mental concentration becomes. Stopping and collecting our mind, we naturally become able to see. In observing, the mind becomes increasingly still. We do not need to search for anything more. We only need to practice the simple exercises proposed by the Buddha in these two sutras.

CHAPTER FIVE

Subjects of Practice

We practice stopping and observing in order to arrive at liberation, freedom from being bound. Bound to what? First of all, to falling into forgetfulness, to losing our mindfulness. We live as if we are in a dream. We are dragged into the past and pulled into the future. We are bound by our sorrows, by holding onto anger, unease, and fear. "Liberation" here means transforming and transcending these conditions in order to be fully awake, at ease and in peace, joyfully and freshly. When we live in this way, our life is worth living, and we become a source of joy to our family and to everyone around us. Buddhism often refers to "emancipation," i.e., going beyond and leaving birth and death behind. We feel threatened by death. How much unease and fear have been brought about by the fear of death! Meditation allows us to be free from these bonds of unease and fear.

Following are seven methods for putting the *Anapanasati Sutta* into practice. They are offered in a simple way, in accord with the spirit of the sutra. Please use whatever methods suit you in your present situation, and practice them first. Although the sixteen exercises of practicing Full Awareness of the Breath are intimately connected to one another, the order in which they are given in the sutra is not necessarily a progression from easy to difficult. Every exercise is as wonderful as every other, as easy and as difficult as every other one. We can, however, say that the preliminary instructions place greater importance on "stopping," and the later ones place more importance on "looking deeply," although, of course, stopping and looking deeply cannot exist separately from one another. If there is stopping, looking deeply is already present, more or less; and if there is looking deeply, there is a natural stopping. The subjects for full awareness suggested below can be divided into seven categories:

1. Following the breath in daily life—eliminating forgetfulness and unnecessary thinking (EXERCISES 1-2)

2. Awareness of the body (EXERCISES 3)

3. Realizing the unity of body and mind (EXERCISES 4)

4. Nourishing ourselves with the joy and happiness of meditation (EXERCISES 5-6)

5. Observing our feelings (EXERCISES 7-8)

6. Caring for and liberating the mind (EXERCISES 9-12)

7. Looking deeply in order to shed light on the true nature of all dharmas (EXERCISES 13-16).

Laypersons as well as monks and nuns must know how to practice both the first subject (following the breath in daily life) and the fourth (nourishing ourselves with the joy of meditation). Every time we practice sitting meditation, we should always begin with these two subjects. Only after that should we go into the other subjects. Every time we notice our state of mind becoming agitated, dispersed, or ill-at-ease, we should practice the fifth subject (observing in order to shine light on our feelings). The seventh subject is the door that opens onto liberation from birth and death, and all those of great understanding have to pass through this door. This subject is the greatest gift the Buddha has given us. The first six subjects all involve stopping as well as looking deeply, but the seventh emphasizes looking deeply. Only after we have the capacity to concentrate our mind with great stability should we embark on this subject.

THE FIRST SUBJECT OF FULL AWARENESS: FOLLOWING THE BREATH IN DAILY LIFE, ELIMINATING FORGETFULNESS AND UNNECESSARY THINKING (EXERCISES 1-2)

"Breathing in, I know I am breathing in. Breathing out, I know I am breathing out."

1. *"Breathing in a long breath, I know I am breathing in a long breath. Breathing out a long breath, I know I am breathing out a long breath."*

2. *"Breathing in a short breath, I know I am breathing in a short breath. Breathing out a short breath, I know I am breathing out a short breath."*

Most readers of this book do not live in forests, under trees, or in monasteries. In our daily lives, we drive cars, wait for buses, work in offices and factories, talk on the telephone, clean our houses, cook meals, wash clothes, and so on. Therefore, it is important that we learn to practice Full Awareness of Breathing during our daily lives. Usually, when we perform these tasks, our thoughts wander, and our joy, sorrow, anger, and unease follow close behind. Although we are alive, we are not able to bring our minds into the present moment, and we live in forgetfulness.

We can begin to enter the present moment by becoming aware of our breath. Breathing in and breathing out, we know we are breathing in and out, and we can smile to affirm that we are in control of ourselves. Through Awareness of Breathing, we can be awake in, and to, the present moment. Being attentive, we already establish "stopping" and concentrating the mind. Full Awareness of our Breathing helps our mind stop wandering in confused, never-ending thoughts.

Most of our daily activities can be accomplished while following our breath according to the exercises in the sutra. When our work demands special attentiveness to avoid confusion or an accident, we can unite Full Awareness of Breathing with the task itself. For example, when we are carrying a pot of boiling water or doing electrical repairs, we can be aware of every movement of our hands, and we can nourish this awareness by means of our breath: "Breathing in, I am aware my hands are carrying a pot of boiling water." "Breathing out, I am aware that my right hand is holding an electrical wire." "Breathing in, I am aware that I am passing another car." "Breathing out, I know that the situation is under control." We can practice like this.

It is not enough to combine Awareness of Breathing only with tasks that require so much attention. We must also combine Full Awareness of our Breathing with every movement of our body: "Breathing in, I am sitting down." "Breathing out, I am wiping the table." "Breathing in, I smile to myself." "Breathing out, I light the stove." Stopping the random progression of thoughts and no longer living in forgetfulness are giant steps forward in our meditation practice. We can realize this by following our breath and combining it with awareness of each daily activity.

There are people who have no peace or joy because they cannot stop their unnecessary thinking. They are forced to take sedatives to fall asleep, but even in their dreams, they continue to feel fears, anxieties, and unease. Thinking too much can give us headaches, and our spiritual power will diminish. By following our breath and combining conscious breathing with our daily activities, we can cut across the stream of disturbing thoughts and light the lamp of awakening. Full Awareness of an out-breath and an in-breath is something wonderful that anyone can practice. Whether or not we live in a monastery or a meditation center, we can practice in this way. Combining Full Awareness of Breathing with full awareness of the movements of our body during daily activities—walking, standing, lying, sitting, working— is a basic practice to cultivate concentration and live in an awakened state. During the first few minutes of sitting meditation, you can use this method to harmonize your breathing, and if it seems necessary, you can continue following your breath with Full Awareness throughout the entire period.

"Breathing in a long breath, I know I am breathing in a long breath. Breathing out a long breath, I know I am breathing out a long breath." (Breathing out, I know my out-breath is a long breath.)

"Breathing in a short breath, I know I am breathing in a short breath. Breathing out a short breath, I know I am breathing out a short breath."

Our breath is usually short at first, but as we practice, our breath slows down and deepens. To practice these two exercises is to know whether our breath is short or long. We do not purposefully make our breath long. We do not say, "I will breathe in a long breath." Strictly speaking, we should say, "Breathing in, I know I am breathing in a long (or a short) breath." We simply recognize when we are breathing in and when we are breathing out. We can abbreviate "Breathing in, I know I am breathing in. Breathing out, I know I am breathing out," to "In, Out." We say these two words silently as we breathe in and out to help our concentration.

In the version of the *Anapananusmrti Sutra* from the Chinese canon that is in Appendix Two, the first of the sixteen breathing exercises is, "Breathing in, I know I am breathing in. Breathing out, I know I am breathing out." The second is, "Breathing in a long breath or a short breath, I know whether it is a long breath or a short breath. Breathing out a long breath or a short breath, I know whether it is a long breath or a short breath." This version is more in accord with the instructions given here, that we should just recognize the length of our breath.

As we continue to follow our breathing, we recognize its quality, "I know I am breathing in, and I know it is a short breath." If it is short, let it be short. It is not important to make it long. This is called "mere recognition." It is the same when we have a painful feeling. The first thing to do is to recognize it. If your breathing is fast, recognize that it is fast. If it is slow, recognize that it is slow. If it is uneven, recognize that it is uneven. If it is even, recognize that it is even. When we begin, our breathing may be uneven, but after a few minutes of practice, it will become even and it will bring us peace and joy. We do not force our breathing to be deep or slow. It is our continued practice that makes our breathing become deep or slow, quite naturally. When we recognize a deep, slow breath, we can say, "Deep," as we breathe in, and "Slow,""as we breathe out. With the first two exercises, the nourishment of the joy of meditation is already present, and once we have it, we can begin to share it with our family and friends. We do not have to wait until we are a Dharma teacher.

THE SECOND SUBJECT OF FULL AWARENESS: AWARENESS OF THE BODY (EXERCISE 3)

3. "Breathing in, I am aware of my whole body. Breathing out, I am aware of my whole body."

With this second subject, we embrace our body with mindfulness rather than just embracing our breathing, as in the first two exercises. We recognize the presence of our body and we "return home" to be one with it. Breathing is the vehicle that brings us home, to our body. If we do not come back to our home and care for it, who will? When we come home to it, our body breathes a sigh of relief and says, "She has come back at last!" We do not blame our body, accusing it of being a nuisance because we have a headache or an upset stomach. We embrace our wounded body, care for it, and heal it with right mindfulness.

In the *Anapanasati Sutta*, the Buddha teaches four exercises in connection with the body, but in the *Satipatthana Sutta* many more methods are taught: (1) Breathing. (2) Recognizing the body, calming the body. (3) Recognizing the positions of the body. When standing, sitting, walking, or lying down, you know you are standing, sitting, walking, or lying down. (4) Recognizing actions of the body: bending down, drinking tea, lifting up a cup of tea. If your actions are hurried and forgetful, you recognize that, and once you do, your hurriedness and forgetfulness will disappear. (5) Observing different parts of the body.

During the practice of meditation, body and mind become unified. In the sitting, lying, standing, or walking position, we practice awareness of our body. We know that the Buddha taught walking meditation. Today, when we practice walking meditation, we can use ideas from the *Anapanasati Sutta* to help us succeed in our walking. If we are walking slowly, as in the meditation hall, we can take one step and say, "In," silently. It means, "Breathing in, I know I am breathing in." For as long as the in-breath lasts, we continue stepping with our left foot. As soon as the out-breath begins, we begin stepping with our right foot and say the word, "Out," silently, which means, "Breathing out, I know I am breathing out." We just take a step and know we are breathing in, and we take a step and know we are breathing out. That is all we need to do. There is nothing else besides that. If we put our whole body and mind into one step, we are successful in walking meditation. After practicing, "In, Out," four or five times, our breath will become deeper and slower quite naturally. We can recognize that and say, "Deep," as we breathe in and, "Slow," as we breathe out. When we practice walking meditation outdoors, rather than taking one breath with each step, we take two or three steps for every breath. For every step, we say, "In," so if we are taking three steps with each in-breath, we say, "In, in, in." And if we take three steps with each out-breath, we say, "Out, out, out." And then, "Deep, deep, deep. Slow, slow, slow."

Sometimes we practice observing different parts of our body, one by one, and then observe the whole body. We can start with our hair, "Aware of my hair, I breathe in. Smiling to my hair, I breathe out," and then we survey all the different parts of our body, down to the tips of our toes. We are in contact with each of them by means of mindfulness. We can practice this meditation when we are sitting or when we are lying down. Hospitals examine patients with a scanner, an instrument that scans the body using a laser beam to help diagnose what is wrong. Mindfulness also scans the body, though not with laser beams. Right mindfulness is a ray of light that recognizes the different parts of our body, helps us become acquainted with them, and shows us how to take care of them. In half an hour, we can scan the thirty-six parts of our body named in the *Satipatthana Sutta*. Medical research confirms that to show this kind of care to the different parts of our body is an important part of healing. You can lie down and guide yourself in this meditation: "Breathing in, I am aware of my eyes. Breathing out, I smile to my eyes," and then do the same for the other parts of your body. If your concentration is strong, you will see how much joy your eyes bring into your life, and that alone will make you feel happy. Seeing how precious your eyes are will help you take good care of them.

During this practice, difficult feelings sometimes arise. For example, you may be observing your heart when suddenly you notice anxiety arising. Perhaps your friend has a heart condition, and you are anxious about that. In any case, do not push the feeling away. Just look at it and say, "Breathing in, I am aware that I am anxious," and then continue observing your body under the supervision of the Full Awareness of Breathing.

Here is another example. As you become aware of your digestive organs, you see millions of minute living beings that are living inside your intestines. Do not push this perception away. Simply remain aware of it, "Breathing in, I am aware of the minute organisms living within me." Your awareness of your symbiotic relationship with these organisms can be a rich subject for meditation. Recognize it as such, and make an appointment with yourself to return to this subject later, and then continue on your journey observing the rest of your body. We call this practice "scanning the body with our awareness."

We generally pay very little attention to the organs of our body unless they cause us pain. We may pass half our life so caught up in our goals and projects that we never even take time to notice our little toe. Our little toe is very important. It has been kind to us for many years. If, one day in the future, there is a sign of cancer in it, what will we do? You may think somehow that being aware of your body is not an important spiritual practice, but that is not correct. Any physiological, psychological, or physical phenomenon can be a door to full realization. If you meditate on your toe, holding your toe between your fingers, that can lead to your goal of realization. The secret of practicing this second subject of Full Awareness, "Awareness of the Body," is to concentrate your mind and observe each organ of the body in full awareness. If you practice this way, one day you will see things in a new way that will change your view and your way of life. The hairs on your head may seem ordinary, but each hair is an ambassador of truth. Please receive the credentials of your hair. Observe them well and discover every message that each hair sends to you. According to the principle of interpenetration, each hair contains all the information of the cosmos. Are your eyes unimportant? Of course not. They are the windows that open up onto the miracle of reality. Don't neglect anything. Look deeply, and you will see. That is the practice of meditation.

THE THIRD SUBJECT OF FULL AWARENESS: REALIZING THE UNITY OF BODY AND MIND (EXERCISE 4)

4. *"Breathing in, I calm my whole body. Breathing out, I calm my whole body."*

Now that we have observed and accepted our whole body, we can bring peace and calm to it. Sometimes our body does not function peacefully. We may work hard and notice that our body is not at peace. When we lie down, we see that our body is shaking from exhaustion. Our breath can be strained as well. When we are angry or exhausted, we may feel our body and our breath coming apart at the seams. We can use this exercise to remind us to take care of our body: "Breathing in, I calm the functions of my body. Breathing out, I calm the functions of my body." Just by concentrating this way, we help our blood circulate better and make the rhythm of our heart more even.

During another period of meditation, we can observe our whole body without discriminating between the parts: "Breathing in, I am aware of my whole body." (EXERCISE 3) At this point, allow your breathing, your body, and your observing mind to all become one. Breathing and body are one. Breathing and mind are one. Mind and body are one. Mind is not an entity that exists independently, outside of our breathing and our body. The boundary between the subject and the object of observation does not actually exist. We observe "the body in the body." The mind is one with the object it is observing. This principle has been developed extensively in Mahayana Buddhism: Subject and object are empty. Subject and object are not two.

If you practice this way for ten or twenty minutes, the flow of your breathing and of your bodily functions will become very calm, and your mind will feel quite released. When you begin to practice, it may seem as rough as coarsely milled wheat, but as you continue practice, the flour will become finer and finer. The fourth breathing exercise accompanies you along this path: "Breathing in, I calm my whole body. Breathing out, I calm my whole body." It is like drinking a glass of cool lemonade on a hot day and feeling your body becoming cool inside. When you breathe in, the air enters your body and calms all the cells of your body. At the same time, each "cell" of your breathing becomes more peaceful and each "cell" of your mind also becomes more peaceful. The three are one, and each one is all three. This is the key to meditation. Breathing brings the sweet joy of meditation to you. It is food. If you are nourished by the sweet joy of meditation, you become joyful, fresh, and tolerant, and everyone around you will benefit from your joy.

Although the aim of the fourth breathing exercise is to bring calmness to the movements of your body, its effect is to bring calmness to your breathing and to your mind also. The calmness of one brings calmness to all three. In the calmness of meditation, discrimination between body and mind no longer exists, and you dwell at rest in the state of "body and mind at one," no longer feeling that the subject of meditation exists outside of the object of meditation.

THE FOURTH SUBJECT OF FULL AWARENESS: NOURISHING OURSELVES WITH THE JOY AND HAPPINESS OF MEDITATION (EXERCISES 5-6)

5. *"Breathing in, I feel joyful. Breathing out, I feel joyful."*

Those who practice meditation should know how to nourish themselves with the joy and happiness of meditative concentration, in order to reach real maturity and help the world. Life in this world is both painful and miraculous. The Buddhist traditions of the Southern schools stress the painful side of life, while those of the Northern schools help us touch and appreciate the marvels of life. The violet bamboo, the yellow chrysanthemum, the white clouds, and the full moon are all wondrous expressions of the Dharmakaya, the body of the Dharma. Our body, even though it is impermanent, without an independent self, and subject to suffering, is also infinitely wondrous. The joy of beginning to meditate is like leaving the busy city, and going off to the countryside to sit under a tree. We feel ourselves filled with peace and joy. What a relief!

At the end of each day, you can sit cross-legged on a cushion or sit on a chair and begin to practice conscious breathing. If you do this, you will feel great joy. This is the initial sensation of the peace and joy of meditation. The fifth breathing exercise helps us touch this sensation. If you can set aside the stresses and difficulties of your day and enter your meditation filled with joy, it is easy to arrive at the state of peace and happiness.

Joy is a positive psychological and physiological state. Joy helps our blood circulate throughout our body, which makes us feel more alive. When we feel joyful, concentration is easy. When we do not feel joyful, it can be difficult to concentrate. When we are concentrated, we see more clearly and have a deeper understanding of things. How can we encourage the feeling of joy? Please try the following exercises:

"Breathing in, I know I have two good eyes. Breathing out, I feel joy."

"Breathing in, I recognize that my liver is in good condition. Breathing out, I feel joy."

"Breathing in, I am aware of my Sangha protecting me. Breathing out, I feel joy."

The last exercise is for those of you who are part of a Sangha, a community of practitioners. Your community may not seem to be doing anything special, but just by its existence, it is protecting you. When you attend a retreat and practice with the Sangha—sitting, eating, walking, breathing together in mindfulness—you feel great security and encouragement. In each session of sitting meditation, you can treat yourself to this kind of practice. Touching joy for twenty or thirty minutes is truly nourishing for your body and mind.

6. "Breathing in, I feel happy. Breathing out, I feel happy."

The sixth exercise allows us to experience happiness as we breathe in and out. Happiness is easiest when our body and mind are at ease, free of excessive worries and preoccupations.

Happiness is more than joy. According to the teachings of the Buddha, joy is less pure because there can be excitement in it. When we anticipate some special occasion, we may say, "I feel very excited. I can't wait." But when we feel too excited, our mind is not at peace. In Chinese, the characters "Peace" and "Joy" often appear together. One student said to me, "I can't wait to hear you teach on Friday!" If we are too excited about something in the future, how can we enjoy what is happening in the present moment? In the West, joy is often equated with excitement. According to the Buddha, joy is not the same as happiness. In the beginning, we need joy. But as we develop our happiness, the excitement that is present in joy disappears.

The example given in the sutra is of a man in the desert, about to die of thirst, who all of a sudden sees an oasis, a pool of water, in the midst of a grove of trees. He feels joy and excitement. His mind and body race towards the pool, and he bends down, puts his hands in the water and brings the water to his mouth. Until the very last moment before he drinks the water, joy is there. His hands are shaking from excitement. But when he finally drinks the water, he tastes real happiness, and his excitement has completely disappeared. The Buddha was not criticizing joy. We need joy very much, but we also need to go further than joy.

In the river of our feelings are many unpleasant ones. We want more than anything for them to change. The Buddha understood this. That is why the first two exercises that he proposed on the subject of feelings are to nourish us with joy and happiness. They are the medicine we need to strengthen us before we try to cure the deepest, most fundamental causes of our sickness. If we endeavor to write down one condition for happiness that exists in our life right now, I think that before long we will fill a whole sheet of paper. Whatever we are doing—sitting meditation, walking meditation, washing, cooking, or cleaning—we can ask ourselves, What are the conditions that we have for happiness? When we see one such condition, we can write it down. According to the *Lotus Sutra,* we are the heirs to many priceless jewels, but we wander around as if we were destitute children.

To succeed in the practice, we must "experience" (Pali: *patisamvedi*) joy and happiness. It is not enough to repeat the words "joy" and "happiness" to ourselves. If we do not use our eyes of understanding and practice right mindfulness, we will not be able to touch the conditions that can bring us joy and happiness in the present moment.

The Buddha taught us to look deeply at pleasant, unpleasant, and neutral feelings. Neutral feelings are those which are neither pleasant nor unpleasant. When we have a toothache, for example, we have an unpleasant feeling. But when we do not have a toothache, we do not enjoy our non-toothache. We think having a non-toothache is a neutral feeling. Having the toothache helps us see that not having a toothache is a very pleasant feeling. Only after we become blind are we aware that having eyes to see the blue sky and the white clouds is a miracle. While we are able to see, we rarely notice. We think seeing is neutral. The fact that we have a Sangha and the opportunity to practice may be just a neutral feeling, but when we are aware how precious a jewel a Sangha is, the feeling is very pleasant. The fact that we are alive is truly a miracle. We could say there is nothing special about it, but when we are deeply aware of being alive in this moment, we see how wonderful, how pleasant it is! Through the practice of meditation, we learn to transform so-called neutral feelings into pleasant ones, that are healthy and long-lasting. Meditation helps us see what is painful and what is miraculous. Happiness in itself is nourishing. It is not necessary to look for happiness outside of ourselves. We only need to be aware of the existence of happiness, and we have it right away. We can enjoy pleasant feelings like the air around us as we need them. Nourished by the happiness of meditation, we become tolerant, at ease and compassionate with ourselves and others, and our happiness is felt by everyone. With peace in ourselves, we can share peace with others, and we have enough strength and patience to face the many hardships in life with patience and perseverance.

THE FIFTH SUBJECT OF FULL AWARENESS: OBSERVING OUR FEELINGS (EXERCISES 7-8)

7. *"Breathing in, I am aware of my mental formations. Breathing out, I am aware of my mental formations."*

Mental formations (Pali: *cittasankhara*) are psychological phenomena. There are fifty-one mental formations according to the Vijñanavada School of the the Mahayana, and fifty-two according to the Theravada. Feelings are one of them. In the seventh and eighth breathing exercises, mental formations simply mean feelings. They do not refer to the other fifty mental formations. In the *Vimutti Magga*, we are told that mental formations in these exercises mean feelings and perceptions. It is more likely that mental formations here simply mean feelings, although feelings are caused in part by our perceptions.

Some feelings are more rooted in the body, such as a toothache or a headache. Feelings that are more rooted in our mind arise from our perceptions. In the early morning when you see the first light of day and hear the birds singing, you might have a very pleasant feeling. But if once at this time of day you received a long-distance telephone call that your parent had suffered a heart attack, the feeling that comes from that perception may be painful for many years.

When you feel sad, do remember that it will not last forever. If someone comes and smiles at you, it may vanish right away. In fact, it has not gone anywhere. It has just ceased to manifest. Two days later, if someone criticizes you, sadness may reappear. Whether the seed of sadness is manifesting or not depends on causes and conditions. Our practice is to be aware of the feeling that is present right now: "Breathing in, I am aware of the feeling that is in me now. Breathing out, I am aware of the feeling that is in me now."

If it is a pleasant feeling, when we are aware that it is a pleasant feeling, it may become even more pleasant. If we are eating or drinking something that is healthy and nourishing for us, our feeling of happiness will grow as we become aware of it. If what we are consuming is harmful for our intestines, our lungs, our liver, or our environment, our awareness will reveal to us that our so-called pleasant feeling has within it many seeds of suffering.

The seventh and eighth breathing exercises help us observe all our feelings—pleasant and unpleasant. Feelings arising from irritation, anger, anxiety, weariness, and boredom are disagreeable ones. Whatever feeling is present, we identify it, recognize that it is there, and shine the sun of our awareness on it.

If we have an unpleasant feeling, we take that feeling in our arms like a mother holding her crying baby. The "mother" is mindfulness and the "crying baby" is the unpleasant feeling. Mindfulness and conscious breathing are able to calm the feeling. If we do not hold the unpleasant feeling in our arms but allow it just to remain in us, it will continue to make us suffer. "Breathing in, I touch the unpleasant feeling in me. Breathing out, I touch the unpleasant feeling in me."

In Buddhist meditation, looking deeply is based on non-duality. Therefore, we do not view irritation as an enemy coming to invade us. We see that we are that irritation in the present moment. When we are irritated, we know, "This irritation is in me. I am this irritation," and we breathe in and out in this awareness. Thanks to this approach, we no longer need to oppose, expel, or destroy our irritation. When we practice looking deeply, we do not set up barriers between good and bad in ourselves and transform ourselves into a battlefield. We treat our irritation with compassion and nonviolence, facing it with our heart filled with love, as if we were facing our own baby sister. We bring the light of awareness to it by breathing in and out mindfully. Under the light of awareness, our irritation is gradually transformed. Every feeling is a field of energy. A pleasant feeling is an energy that can nourish. Irritation is a feeling that can destroy. Under the light of awareness, the energy of irritation can be transformed into a kind of energy that nourishes us.

Feelings originate either in the body or in our perceptions. When we suffer from insomnia, we feel fatigue or irritation. That feeling originates in our body. When we misperceive a person or an object, we may feel anger, disappointment, or irritation. This feeling originates in our perception. According to Buddhism, our perceptions are often inaccurate and cause us to suffer. The practice of Full Awareness is to look deeply in order to see the true nature of everything and to go beyond our inaccurate perceptions. Seeing a rope as a snake, we may cry out in fear. Fear is a feeling, and mistaking the rope for a snake is an inaccurate perception.

If we live our daily lives in moderation, keeping our bodies in good health, we can diminish painful feelings which originate in the body. By observing each thing clearly and opening the boundaries of our understanding, we can diminish painful feelings that originate from perceptions. When we observe a feeling deeply, we recognize the multitude of causes near and far that helped bring it about, and we discover the very nature of feeling.

When a feeling of irritation or fear is present, we can be aware of it, nourishing our awareness through breathing. With patience, we come to see more deeply into the true nature of this feeling, and in seeing, we come to understand, and understanding brings us freedom. The seventh exercise refers to the awareness of a mental formation, namely a feeling. When we have identified the feeling we can see how it arises, exists for a while, and ceases to be in order to become something else.

8. "Breathing in, I calm my mental formations. Breathing out, I calm my mental formations."

We use our conscious breathing in order to calm and transform the energy of our feeling. It is like riding a bicycle. As long as we continue to pedal, we will move forward, but as soon as we stop, we will lose our balance and fall off. We have to keep following our breathing for the feeling to calm and transform. If you have an unpleasant feeling but do not know what to do to look after it, you are not as wise as the mother who, when she hears her baby crying, picks it up in her arms right away.

"Hello, sadness. Come here. I shall look after you." We care for our sadness by breathing mindfully as we sit, walk, or lie in the grass. We can teach children how to look after their feelings of fear or anger by showing them how to be aware of the rising and falling of their abdomen as they breathe. When the child becomes afraid or angry, if she has forgotten the exercise you showed her, you only have to remind her how to practice. In the same way, when you live with a Sangha, your fellow practitioners will remind you to practice when you are overcome by strong emotions.

By observing the true nature of any feeling, we can transform its energy into the energy of peace and joy. When we understand someone, we can accept and love him, and there is no longer any feeling of reproach or irritation against him. The energy of the feeling of irritation, in this case, has been transformed into the energy of love. The Buddha had much love and compassion as far as the body and the feelings of people are concerned. He wanted his disciples to return to, look after, care for, heal, and nourish their bodies and minds. How deeply the Buddha understood human beings!

THE SIXTH SUBJECT OF FULL AWARENESS: CARING FOR AND LIBERATING THE MIND (EXERCISES 9-12)

9. *"Breathing in, I am aware of my mind. Breathing out, I am aware of my mind."*

The ninth breathing exercise is the one that recognizes the other mental formations besides feelings. It is the first of the group of four exercises that belong to the field of the mind. In the Sutra on the Four Establishments of Mindfulness, we are taught to observe "the mind in the mind." It means we should observe mental formations in the spirit of non-duality, with no barrier between the subject and object of observation. When we look at the blue sky, the boundary between the observer and the infinite blue of the sky disappears, and we feel a deep contact between ourselves and the blue sky. When a grain of salt standing next to the sea asks, "How salty is the sea?", he is told that the only way to know is to jump into the sea and become one with it.

Mind (citta) here is composed of psychological phenomena, including perception, thinking, reasoning, discriminating, imagining, and all the activities that have their roots in the subconscious. As soon as any psychological phenomenon (a mental formation, cittasamskara) arises, we should breathe in and out and identify it. As we continue to observe it, we can see its connection with the whole of our mind. The meaning of the ninth breathing exercise is: "I breathe in and out and identify the mental formation that is present at this moment in me."

To identify a mental formation with the help of conscious breathing means to recognize, embrace, and become one with that mental formation. It does not mean to drown in that mental formation, because the subject that is recognizing, embracing, and becoming one with the mental formation is the energy of mindfulness. When our mindfulness is one with the mental formation, the mental formation quite naturally changes for the better.

The first four breathing exercises help us become one with our breathing and drop all thinking, discriminating ideas, and imaginings. The second four exercises get us in touch with our feelings. The ninth exercise helps us identify psychological phenomena, such as thoughts or imaginings, as they arise. The term "citta" includes all psychological phenomena, such as feelings, perceptions, thoughts, reasoning, and so forth, along with their objects. It does not refer to a single, unchangeable psychological subject. Mind is a river of psychological phenomena that is always flowing. In this river, the arising, duration, and cessation of any phenomenon is always linked with the arising, duration, and cessation of all other phenomena. To know how to identify psychological phenomena as they arise and develop is an important part of meditation practice. When we recognize the mental formation that is manifesting in us, we recognize whether it is wholesome or unwholesome. Attachment, aversion, ignorance, pride, suspicion and being caught in views are unwholesome, and they cause us to suffer. When we suspect someone of committing a wrongdoing, whether it is our teacher or our friends on the path, we suffer. When we doubt the teachings and have no confidence in anyone around us, we suffer a lot. We can only practice when we have faith and confidence. Pride is a great hindrance to progress. We think that we are better than others, that only we can see the truth. That is not at all conducive to peace and joy.

The activities of our mind, often unstable and agitated, are like a torrent of water washing over the rocks. In traditional Buddhist literature, mind is often compared to a monkey always swinging from branch to branch or to a horse galloping out of control. Once our mind is able to identify what is happening, we will be able to see clearly our mental formation and make it calm. Just that will bring us peace, joy, and stillness.

10. *"Breathing in, I make my mind happy. Breathing out, I make my mind happy."*

The tenth breathing exercise is intended to gladden our mind. Compare this with the fifth and sixth exercises. The fifth aims at the experience of joy, and the sixth aims at the experience of happiness. These three methods can bring us to the land of great bliss, to a state of relaxation in meditative concentration. To better succeed in the practice of the tenth exercise we must know how to recognize and touch the positive mental formations that are already present in us, such as faith, goodwill, compassion, understanding, tolerance, and equanimity. Our mind becomes joyful every time we recognize these positive mental formations.

This state brings us ease and can nourish the power of our concentration. The Buddha wants us to be nourished by feelings of peace and joy. To gladden the mental formations (as the tenth breathing exercise is sometimes expressed) or to make the mind happy is to see the beneficial mental formations that are within us. For instance, to have faith and confidence in the path we are following is beneficial. To know what it is right to do and not to do is also beneficial. For instance, if I see others practicing sitting meditation and I recognize that it is a good thing to do, I will have the intelligence to join them. If I do not want to kill a slug or caterpillar that is eating the lettuce in my garden because I have the wholesome mental formation of nonviolence, I will know to go out with a flashlight while it is still dark and gently remove the slugs and caterpillars from the lettuce plants and put them somewhere else. Or I may decide to be a vegetarian because I do not feel happy about factory farming, the slaughter of animals, or the death from starvation of thousands of children because there is not enough grain for human consumption. These decisions arise from the mental formation of nonviolence in me. There are ways you can practice the tenth breathing exercise during sitting meditation: "Breathing in, I recognize the mental formation of nonviolence in me. Breathing out, I feel happy." "Breathing in, I have faith in the practice I am doing. Breathing out, I feel happy." "Breathing in, I know that at this moment I am not caught in any desire. Breathing out, I feel happy." "Breathing in, I know that I am not angry at anyone. Breathing out, I feel happy." But we should not stop at this. We can continue by "observing the mental formation to shed light on it," in order to arrive at an awakened understanding. Only awakened understanding can lead us to complete freedom.

11. *"Breathing in, I concentrate my mind. Breathing out, I concentrate my mind."*

The eleventh method aims at concentrating our mind on a single object. We bring all our power of concentration and place it on the mental formation that is present. Concentration means to direct the energy of our mind towards one object. It is called ekagatta in Pali, which means "one-pointedness." The mental formation that is manifesting in our mind at that moment is a unique object, such as faith. We are in touch with that mental formation. We recognize it and we call it by its name. Through this practice the energy of joy arises, and our faith develops. If the mental formation is negative, we also recognize it and call it by its name, directing all our mental energy upon it. We embrace it and look deeply at it, and doing this already begins the work of transforming that negative mental formation. It is like waking up on a cold morning and lighting a fire. The cold air is warmed by the warm air of the fire. We do not need to open the door and force the cold air to go outside to make the room warm. All we have to do is tend the fire. In the case of a negative mental formation, all we have to do is look after it with the warmth of the fire of our mindfulness. Only by concentrating steadily on an object can we observe it. The object of our mind is lit up by our observation, like a performer standing in a spotlight on a stage. The object might be moving in time and space, since it is alive. But our mind is also alive, and in the state of concentration, subject and object become one.

Breathing is an object of our concentrated mind. We put all our attention on our breath, and our mind and our breath become one. That is concentration. After practicing with the breath, we can practice with other physiological, psychological, and physical phenomena. Only if there is concentration can the work of looking deeply take place.

12. *"Breathing in, I liberate my mind. Breathing out, I liberate my mind."*

The twelfth exercise aims at untying all the knots of the mind—the sorrows and memories of the past, the anxieties and predictions concerning the future, feelings of irritation, fear, and doubt in the present, or confusion created by inaccurate perceptions. Only by concentrating the mind do we have the capacity to observe, illumine, and be emancipated from obstacles.

When we say, "liberate my mind," mind here refers to any mental formation that makes us anxious, makes us suffer, or pushes us in the wrong direction. We open our mind so the light of concentration will reveal what is there and liberate what is there. It is the same as trying to untie knots in thread. We have to be calm, and we need to take time. By observing our mind in all its subtlety, in a calm and self-contained way, we can free our mind from all confusion. "Breathing in, I open my heart for all the knots to be untied. Breathing out, I open my heart for all the knots to be untied."

THE SEVENTH SUBJECT OF FULL AWARENESS:
LOOKING DEEPLY IN ORDER TO SHED LIGHT
ON THE TRUE NATURE OF ALL DHARMAS
(EXERCISES 13-16)

13. "Breathing in, I observe the impermanent nature of all dharmas. Breathing out, I observe the impermanent nature of all dharmas."

The thirteenth breathing exercise proposed by the Buddha aims at looking deeply to shed light on the impermanent nature of all dharmas. All phenomena, whether physiological, psychological, or physical, without exception, are impermanent. The meditation to look deeply at the impermanent nature of all phenomena is one of the basic practices. If we hear someone talking about impermanence, we may think we understand. But understanding impermanence is not a matter of words or concepts, but a matter of practice. Only through our daily practice of stopping and looking deeply can we experience the truth of impermanence. Impermanent does not only mean, "Here today, gone tomorrow." The meditation on impermanence is a deep, penetrating, and wonderful path of meditation. There is no phenomenon whatsoever with a separate, lasting individuality. All things are in endless transformation, and all things are without an independent self. To be impermanent is to be without self (anatman). This is a fundamental recognition in Buddhism regarding the nature of all that exists. "Breathing in, I am looking deeply at some object. Breathing out, I observe the impermanent nature of that object." The object I am observing might be a flower, a leaf, or a living being. Looking deeply this way, we can see that change is taking place in every instant. The Sanskrit word for instant is ksana, the shortest unit of time. One second contains many ksana. The first kind of impermanence is called ksana-anitya, "impermanence in every instant." When something reaches the end of a cycle of arising, duration, and cessation, there is a marked change. This second kind of impermanence is called "cyclic impermanence." When we heat water, the water is getting hotter all the time. That is ksana-anitya. Then, suddenly, we see steam. The appearance of steam is a cyclic impermanence of water.

We have to look deeply at cyclic change in order to accept it as a necessary part of life, and not be surprised or suffer so greatly when it occurs. We look deeply at the impermanence of our own body, the impermanence of the things around us, the impermanent nature of the people we love, and the impermanent nature of those who cause us to suffer. If we do not look deeply at impermanence, we may think of it as a negative aspect of life, because it takes away from us the things we love. But looking deeply, we see that impermanence is neither negative nor positive. It is just impermanence. Without impermanence, life would not be possible. Without impermanence, how could we hope to transform our suffering and the suffering of our loved ones into happiness? Without impermanence, how can we hope that a tyrannical regime might become democratic?

Impermanence also means interdependence, that there is no independent individual because everything is changing all the time. A flower is always receiving non-flower elements like water, air, and sunshine, and it is always giving something to the universe. A flower is a stream of change, and a person is also a stream of change. At every instant, there is input and output. When we look deeply at the flower, we see that it is always being born and always dying, and that it is not independent of other things. The components of the universe depend on one another for their existence. In the *Majjhima Nikaya*, it says, "This is, because that is. This is not, because that is not." Impermanence also means "signlessness" (alaksana). The reality of all that exists is beyond every concept and linguistic expression. We cannot go directly to their essential and true nature, because we are accustomed to grasping phenomena through the intermediaries of perception and thought. The categories of perception and thought are "signs."

The example of wave and water is often given to help us understand the "signless" nature of all that exists. A wave can be high or low, can arise or disappear, but the essence of the wave—water—is neither high nor low, neither arising nor disappearing. All signs—high, low, arising, disappearing—cannot touch the essence of water. We cry and laugh according to the sign, because we have not yet seen the essence. The essence (*svabhava*) is the very nature of everything that is, and it is the reality of ourselves. If we only see the wave with its manifestations of being born and dying, we will suffer. But if we see the water, which is the basis of the wave, and see that all the waves are returning to the water, we have nothing to fear. When we begin the practice, we want things to be permanent and we think things have a separate self. Whenever things change, we suffer. To help us not suffer, the Buddha gave us the truths of impermanence and non-self as keys. When we look deeply at the impermanent and non-self nature of all things, we are using those keys to open the door to reality, or *nirvana*. Then our fears and our suffering disappear, and we do not mind whether we are young or old, or even alive or dead. We realize that we do not die in the usual sense of having existed and then ceasing to exist. We see that all of life is ongoing transformation.

"Breathing in, I see the nature of impermanence. Breathing out, I see the nature of impermanence." We have to practice this many times to have success in the practice. We have to practice on our own and with a community, not just during sitting meditation but in whatever we are doing—watering the garden, washing the dishes, walking up and down the stairs, and so on. The reality of everything that exists is its signlessness, since it is a reality that cannot be grasped by concepts and words. Because it cannot be grasped, it is called empty. Emptiness here does not mean nonexistent as opposed to existent. It means signless, free from all imprisonment by concepts—birth/death, existent/nonexistent, increasing/decreasing, pure/impure. This is developed in the fifteenth breathing exercise.

It says in the *Prajñaparamita Heart Sutra*, "All dharmas are marked with emptiness; they are neither produced nor destroyed, neither defiled nor immaculate, neither increasing nor decreasing." Impermanence also means aimlessness (apranihita). The presence of everything that exists is not to attain a final goal. We cannot add on to the true nature of all that exists, nor can we remove anything from it. It has no origin and no end. We do not need to seek realization outside of all that exists. In the very "stuff" of every dharma, the awakened nature is already fully present.

14. "Breathing in, I observe the disappearance of desire. Breathing out, I observe the disappearance of desire."

The fourteenth breathing exercise aims at looking deeply in order to shed light on the true nature of all dharmas and the true nature of our desire.[43] We see that happiness does not lie in ideas about what we will realize in the future, and for that reason we are no longer attached to the objects of our desire that we thought would bring us future happiness. When people go fishing, they sometimes use synthetic bait. The fish thinks the bait is real and bites. If the fish knew that the bait was synthetic, it would never bite, because it would know that it will only lead to suffering. When you have the thought, "If I could only have that, I would be happy," it is a good time to practice the fourteenth breathing exercise.

Many people think that if they do not have a Ph.D. degree, they cannot possibly be happy. Why do you have to have a degree to be happy? It is only because you have an idea that you think so. It is quite possible that after you have a degree, you will still not be happy. The idea that marriage or divorce are the only things that can bring happiness are also just ideas. There is no guarantee that after we have married or divorced, we will have happiness for the rest of our lives. In fact, it could be quite the opposite.

If we can see that the nature of the object of our desire is always changing and on the way to dissolution, our desire for it to be always the same will disappear. A rose, a cloud, a human body, an ancient tree, all are on the way to dissolution. All dharmas pass through the stages of birth, duration, transformation, and disappearance. The beginning practitioner should observe clearly the impermanent and fading nature of all things, including the Five Aggregates that comprise his or her own self. The Nine Contemplations were a special practice used at the time of the Buddha. In them, we observe the decomposition of a corpse from the time it becomes bloated to the time when it disappears into dust and ashes. In *Lessons in Emptiness*, King Trần Thái Tông of thirteenth century Vietnam contemplates as follows:

> Formerly glowing cheeks and pink lips,
> today cold ashes and white bones.
> Position, renown though unsurpassed,
> they are but part of a long dream.
> However rich and noble you are,
> you are no less impermanent.
> Jealousy, pride, and self-clinging,
> but self is always empty.
> Great strength, ability, and success,
> but in them is no final truth.
> Since the four elements come apart,
> why discriminate old from young?
> Crevices erode even mountains,
> more quickly the hero is dead.
> Black hair has hardly grown on our head,
> when suddenly it has turned white.
> Our well-wisher has just departed,
> a mourner arrives on our death.
> This six-foot skeleton of dry bones—
> with what effort it seeks riches.
> This wrapping of skin containing blood
> suffers year after year just because of attachment.

This is a way of looking at our body, and it is also a way of seeing how our mind, so subtle and quick today, can become slow and senile tomorrow. Rivers, mountains, houses, riches, health—all should be meditated on like this. The objects of our desire are all deceptive in appearance. In the light of deep looking, they are no different from the plastic bait containing a dangerous hook inside. Once their true nature is revealed, our desires vanish.

Perhaps you will smile and say that this contemplation is intended principally to bring us to a pessimistic state of mind, frustrating our love of life. This is both true and not true. Medicine may be bitter, but it can heal our sickness. Reality may be cruel, but to see things as they are is the only way to heal ourselves. Reality is the ground of effective liberation. Life passes so quickly, and there is no stopping it from being cut off. The lifeblood of joy flows in every living thing, from the mineral world through the vegetable world, to the world of living beings. Only because we imprison ourselves in the idea of a small self do we create a state of darkness, narrowness, anxiety, and sorrow. According to our narrow view of a truly existing self, life is just my body, my house, my spouse, my children, and my riches. But if we can extend beyond every limit we have created for ourselves, we will see that our life exists in everything, and that the deterioration of phenomena cannot touch that life, just as the arising and disappearing of the waves cannot influence the existence of the water. By observing in this way to shed light on the deterioration of everything, we can smile in the face of birth and death and attain great peace and joy in this life.

15. "Breathing in, I observe cessation. Breathing out, I observe cessation."

The fifteenth exercise helps us free ourselves from individuality, so that we can become part of the whole universe. Cessation in Pali and Sanskrit is nirodha. It means cessation of all erroneous ideas, of all notions that keep us from directly experiencing the ultimate reality, and of all suffering born of our ignorance. That means the cessation of ideas like birth and death, permanence and annihilation, increasing and decreasing, being and nonbeing, coming and going. We have to go beyond these ideas because they form the basis of our suffering, which is expressed as desire and attachment, fear and anxiety, hatred and anger. When we stop having ideas like that, we are in touch with the wonderful true nature of how things are. How can we get beyond our ideas of birth and death, coming and going? First we have to see that things are impermanent; they manifest and pass away. Then we are free to look more deeply and see that reality is beyond all ideas. It is like a coin. At first we see that it has two sides, but when we look more deeply we see that both sides of the coin are made from the same metal. The essence of the coin is the metal. The two sides both arise from the metal. In the same way, birth and death, coming and going, being and nonbeing, permanence and annihilation all arise from the same essence.

16. "Breathing in, I observe letting go. Breathing out, I observe letting go."

The sixteenth exercise, like the fifteenth, aims at helping us look deeply in order to shed light on giving up desire and attachment, fear and anxiety, hatred and anger. Usually we think that if we let go, we will lose the things that make us happy. But the more we let go, the happier we become.

We should not think that letting go means letting go of everything. We do not let go of reality. We let go of all our wrong perceptions about reality. If we cannot let go of our wrong ideas, we cannot enter the world of reality. According to Tang Hôi, letting go means first of all letting go of ideas concerning self and life span. We have an idea that we began to exist the day our mother gave us birth, and the day we are buried, we cease to exist. We say we are our body, and outside of our own body we do not exist. "Breathing in, I let go of my idea of my body as myself." "Breathing out I let go of my idea that this period of fifty to one hundred years is my life span."

When Anathapindika, the lay disciple of the Buddha, was about to pass away and was in great pain he was given teachings by the Venerable Sariputra to help him let go of ideas of self and life span. These teachings can be found in the *Sutra on Teachings to Be Given to the Sick*. After Sariputra guided Anathapindika in a meditation on the Buddha, the Dharma, and the Sangha, to nourish the seeds of joy in him, he began to offer the cream of the Buddha's teachings: "Friend Anathapindika, please meditate like this: 'These eyes are not me. I am not caught in these eyes.'" He went from eyes to ears, nose, tongue, body and mind; to form sound, smell, taste, touch and objects of mind; then to eye consciousness, up to mind consciousness. "All these things are not me. I have no need to be caught by them." Anathapindika was a layman who had given a lot of support to the Buddha and the community of monks.

Sariputra continued, "Friend Anathapindika, all things exist because of causes and conditions. When the causes and conditions for them cease to exist, they no longer exist. The true nature of things is not to be born and not to die, not to come and not to go." When Anathapindika heard these teachings, he understood them immediately. He knew he had only a short time left to live, and that was enough motivation for him to put the teachings into practice without delay. When he practiced in this way, tears of happiness started to run down his cheeks, and Anathapindika passed away in peace. We, too, are fortunate to have the cream of the teachings available to us. We have to practice letting go of our ideas in order to see life everywhere, beyond space and time. Dear reader, do not wait until your last moments to practice this sutra. Practice it now so you can see that you are not enclosed in your small shell of your body or the small shell of your life span.

When we see that there is already a precious jewel in our pocket, we give up every attitude of craving or coveting. Seeing that we are lions, we do not long to nurse from a mother deer. Seeing that we are the sun, we give up the candle's habit of fearing the wind. Seeing that life has no boundaries, we give up all imprisoning divisions. We see ourselves and our life everywhere. That is why we vow to help all living phenomena, all living species, like a bodhisattva who has attained great awakening.

Letting go does not mean abandoning one thing in order to seek something else. It means giving up every comparison, seeing that there is nothing to be removed and nothing to be added, and that the boundary between ourselves and others is not real. We need not give up our human condition in order to become a buddha. We seek buddhahood in our very human condition, giving up nothing and seeking nothing. That is the meaning of apranihita, "aimlessness," sometimes translated as "wishlessness." It is the same as not-seeking, a concept fully developed in Mahayana Buddhism. Let go in order to be everything and to be completely free. Many people have already done so, and each of us can do so also, if we have the intention.

In summary, the order of the Sixteen Breathing Exercises is the order of the Four Establishments of Mindfulness: body, feelings, mind, and objects of mind. The intelligent practitioner knows how to regulate and master his or her breath, body, and mind, in order to enhance the power of concentration before proceeding in the work of looking deeply to shed light. Meditation practice is nourishing for body and mind, and can also expand our vision. Expanded vision enables us to go beyond passionate attachment or aversion to life. It makes us joyful, calm, stable, tolerant, and compassionate. For the practices of the *Sutra on the Full Awareness of Breathing* to have a greater chance of success, the reader is asked to study and practice the Buddha's teachings in the *Sutra on the Four Establishments of Mindfulness* as well.[44]

Appendices

Guided Meditations

Following are some ways for you to guide yourself or each other in sitting meditation, based on the exercises in the *Anapanasati Sutta* offered by the Buddha. You can practice each exercise for as long as you need in order to realize its meaning. You might like to practice one exercise for as long as ten minutes. If the practice is enjoyable and you feel nourished by practicing, you know you are practicing correctly.

The words in parentheses after each exercise are abbreviations of the exercise for you to recall easily the subject of your meditation. You do not have to practice all the exercises here during one sitting.

1. "Breathing in, I know I am breathing in. Breathing out, I know I am breathing out." (In, Out)

2. "Breathing in, my breath goes deep. Breathing out, my breath goes slow." (Deep, Slow)

3. " Breathing in, I am aware of my whole body. Breathing out, I calm my whole body." (Aware of my body, Calming my body)

4. "Breathing in, I know I am alive. Breathing out, I feel the joy of being alive." (Alive, Joy of being alive)

5. "Breathing in, I know I have the opportunity to meditate. Breathing out, I feel happy to have that opportunity." (Opportunity to meditate, Happy)

6. "*Breathing in, I am embracing my unpleasant feeling. Breathing out, I am calming my feeling.*" (*Embracing my feeling, Calming my feeling*)

7. "*Breathing in, I am aware of right mindfulness in me. Breathing out, it makes me happy.*" (*Wholesome mental formation, I am happy*)

8. "*Breathing in, I concentrate on a mental formation which is present. Breathing out, I look deeply at that mental formation.*" (*Concentrate on mental formation, Look deeply at it*)

9. "*Breathing in, I open up my mind to look deeply at my fear. Breathing out, there is liberation from fear.*" (*Opening up my mind, Liberation*)

10. "*Breathing in, I observe a flower. Breathing out, I contemplate the impermanence of the flower.*" (*Observing a flower, Contemplating its impermanence*)

11. "*Breathing in, I look deeply at the object of my desire. Breathing out, I see the disappearance of desire with regard to that object.*" (*Object of desire, Disappearance of desire*)

12. "*Breathing in, I observe the coming and going of the wave. Breathing out, I contemplate the no-coming, no-going of the water.*" (*Coming and going of the wave, No-coming, no-going of the water*)

13. "*Breathing in, I let go of the idea that this body is me. Breathing out, I am not caught in this body.*" (*This body not me, I am not caught in this body*)

14. "*Breathing in, I let go of the idea that I did not exist before I was born. Breathing out, I let go of the idea that I will not exist after I die.*" (*I am not born, I do not die*)

In the second exercise, do not force your breathing to become deeper or slower. This is an exercise of mere recognition. Your breath has actually become deeper and slower as the result of practicing the first exercise. In the third exercise, because of your awareness of your body, you will know how calm it is and you will know what bodily factors need calming. In the fourth and fifth exercises, you do not want to repeat the words "joy" and "happy" without giving them a content. Here we have chosen the fact that you are alive and the fact that you have the chance to meditate as being occasions for your happiness, but you can find other reasons for joy and happiness and substitute them in this exercise. The first five breathing exercises are intended to calm, stop, focus, concentrate, and nourish us. Without these elements in your sitting meditation practice, you will tire of sitting. Only when you feel happy can you have concentration. You cannot achieve concentration by forcing yourself to concentrate.

Methods seven and eight in the *Anapanasati Sutta* become one breathing exercise here, number six. You are aware of an unpleasant feeling or a pleasant feeling that has the capacity to poison or excite you, and you calm these feelings. In the seventh exercise, your mind feels happy because you know that in your consciousness is the capacity to realize wholesome mental formations. The capacity to be mindful, caring, and loving is within everyone. The first seven exercises here cover the first ten methods of the *Anapanasati Sutta*, and they are to nourish and to calm.

In exercise eight, you concentrate your mind on a mental formation. It could be wholesome, unwholesome, or neutral. When you concentrate, you have to concentrate on something; and when you are liberated, you have to be liberated from something. It is not fruitful to repeat the words "concentration" and "liberation" without there being an object for your concentration. When you concentrate and look deeply at a mental formation, you can see why it is there, and that understanding will help you be liberated from it. To open up your mind and liberate your mind in exercise nine, you need to have developed concentration in exercise eight. Exercises eight and nine are an opportunity for us to look at the mental formations that make us suffer.

In exercise ten, you can observe any phenomenon: yourself, another person, or an object in order to contemplate impermanence. Here we have chosen to observe a flower. Buddhist monks and nuns meditate every day on the impermanence of their own person.

In exercise eleven, you should meditate on a specific object of desire. It can be a person or a thing. If a person has become the object of your desire, it can be unpleasant for them if they feel they are losing their freedom. This exercise can help you not be caught in wanting to possess or dominate others. Desire disappears when you see that the true nature of the object you desire is impermanent, has no separate self, and cannot be grasped. If you are not satisfied with what is available in the present moment, you will never be satisfied by attaining what you think will bring you happiness in the future.

In exercise twelve, you contemplate the cessation of ideas concerning birth and death, coming and going, high and low, using the images of water and wave to help you.

In exercise thirteen, you contemplate that this body is not you, and that these feelings, perceptions, mental formations, and consciousness are not you either. The vegetation, the air, and the water are constantly contributing to this body. Feelings and perceptions are dependent on your education, your ancestry, your friends, your teacher and your upbringing. Consciousness is a vast field containing all the seeds with constant output and constant input.

In exercise fourteen, you have to see very clearly the reason for not being born and for not dying. Your so-called birthday was not the day you began to exist. You were in your parents before that, and prior to that in a line of ancestors. After death, you will continue in the clouds and in the dust that is part of the Earth, and in the descendants of your blood family and in your spiritual heirs.

Anapananusmrti Sutras

Translated from the Chinese by Thich Nhat Hanh from the Samyukta Agama (Tsa A Han, chapter 29, Taisho Revised Tripitaka, number 99)

I

This is what I heard. At that time the Buddha was staying in the Jeta grove in Anathapindika's park in the town of Sravasti during the rainy-season retreat. At that time, many elder disciples were spending the retreat with the Blessed One. There were bhiksus staying all around where the Blessed One was, at the roots of trees or in caves. The number of young bhiksus present during that retreat was also quite great. They came to where the Buddha was staying, prostrated at his feet, and then withdrew and sat down to one side. The Buddha gave teachings to the young bhiksus on many subjects, instructing them, teaching them, enlightening them, and delighting them. After giving these teachings, the Lord was silent. When the young bhiksus had heard these teachings from the Buddha, they felt great joy. They stood up, prostrated to the Lord, and withdrew. After that the young bhiksus approached the elders. When they had paid respects to the elder monks, they sat down to one side. At this time, the elder monks thought to themselves, We should take charge of these young monks and give them teachings. Some of us can instruct one monk, others can instruct two or three monks or even more. They put this idea into practice immediately. Some elders taught one young monk, others taught two or three young monks, and others again instructed more than three young monks. There were elders who guided and instructed up to sixty young bhiksus.

At that time when it was the end of the retreat and time for the Inviting Ceremony, the World-Honored One looked over the assembly of bhiksus and told them, "Well done, well done. I am very happy to see you doing the things that are right and fitting for bhiksus to do. Please continue to study and practice diligently like this, and please stay here in Sravasti for another month, until the full-moon day of the month of Komudi."

When many bhiksus who had been spending the rainy-season retreat scattered about in the countryside heard that the World-Honored One would stay at Sravasti until the full-moon day of Komudi, they performed the Inviting Ceremony, finished sewing their robes, and without delay took their robes and bowl and left for the town of Sravasti. When they came to the Anathapindika Monastery, they put away their robes and bowl, washed their feet, and went to the place where the Buddha was sitting. They paid their respects to the Buddha and then withdrew a little and sat down to one side. Then the World-Honored One taught the Dharma to the monks who had just arrived from the surrounding areas. He instructed them on many topics, enlightening and delighting them. When he finished, he sat in silence. When the monks from the surrounding areas heard the teachings, they were delighted. They stood up and prostrated, and then went to the elders. After they paid their respects to these monks, they withdrew a little and sat down to one side. At this time the elder monks thought to themselves, We should also accept the monks who have just come from the surrounding areas, and each of us can instruct one monk, or two monks, or three monks, or more than three monks. They put this idea into practice immediately. There were elders who taught just one of the newly arrived bhiksus, and there were elders who taught more. There were even elders who instructed up to sixty newly arrived bhiksus. The elders did the work of instructing and encouraging the bhiksus who came from the surrounding regions, teaching them everything in order, putting first what should go first and adding later what should be taught later, in a very skillful fashion.

When the day of the full moon came after the Uposatha observances had been performed, the World-Honored One sat before the assembly of monks. After he had cast his gaze over the whole community of bhiksus, he said, "Well done. Well done, bhiksus! I am delighted to see that you have done and are doing the things that are right and fitting for a bhiksu to do. I am very happy when I see you have done and are doing the things that are necessary for a bhiksu to do. Bhiksus, the Buddhas of the past also had communities of bhiksus who did the things that are right and fitting for a bhiksu to do. The Buddhas of the future will also have communities of bhiksus like this community of bhiksus, and they also will do the things that are right and fitting for a bhiksu to do as you today are doing and have done.

"In this community of bhiksus, there are, among the elders, those who have accomplished the first *dhyana*, the second dhyana, the third dhyana, and the fourth dhyana. There are those who have accomplished the *maitri samadhi* (concentration of loving kindness), the *karuna samadhi* (concentration of compassion), the *mudita samadhi* (concentration of joy) and the *upeksa samadhi* (concentration of equanimity). There are those who have realized the limitless-space concentration, the limitless-consciousness concentration, the concentration of no thing exists, and the concentration of no perception and no non-perception. There are those who are always able to remain in one of these samadhis. There are those who have untied the three basic internal knots and have attained the fruit of stream-enterer. They have no fear of falling into the paths of great suffering and are firmly on the way to perfect enlightenment. They only need to return seven times more to be born in the worlds of gods and men before being liberated from the suffering of birth and death. There are monks who, after they have untied the three basic internal knots and have nearly transformed the three poisons of craving, hatred, and ignorance, have realized the fruit of once-returner. There are monks who have untied the first five internal knots and have realized the fruit of non-returning. They are able to reach nirvana in this life and do not need to be born again in the world, which is subject to birth and death. There are bhiksus who have realized the immeasurable miraculous intelligence and even in this world are able to use the divine eye, the divine ear, knowing others' minds, recollection of previous births, knowing others' previous births, and ending all the *asravas*. There are monks who, thanks to practicing the meditation on impurity, have transformed the energy of attachment; thanks to the meditation on loving kindness, have transformed the energy of hatred; thanks to looking deeply at impermanence, have transformed the energy of pride; and thanks to the practice of conscious breathing, have been able to put an end to the [ignorance and suffering that arise in the fields of] feelings and perceptions.

"Bhiksus, what is the way to practice conscious breathing so that we eliminate the [ignorance and the suffering in the fields of] feelings and perceptions?"

—*Samyukta Agama, Sutta No. 815 translated from the Chinese*

II

"A bhiksu who practices the method of conscious breathing very diligently will realize a state of peace and calm in his body and in his mind. Conscious breathing will lead to right mindfulness, the ability to look deeply, and a clear and single-minded perception, so that he is in a position to realize all the Dharma doors that give rise to the fruit of nirvana.

"A bhiksu who lives near a small village or a town puts on his *sanghati* robe in the morning, picks up his bowl and goes into the inhabited area to seek alms. All the time he skillfully guards his six senses and establishes himself in mindfulness. After he has received alms, he returns to his place of abode, takes off his sanghati robe, puts down his bowl, and washes his feet. Then he goes into the forest and sits at the foot of a tree or sits in an empty room or out in the open air. He sits very straight, maintaining mindfulness before him. He lets go of all his cravings. He calms and clarifies his body and mind. He eliminates the five hindrances—craving, anger, dullness, agitation, and suspicion—and all the other afflictions that can weaken his understanding and create obstacles for him in his progress towards nirvana. Then he practices as follows:

1. 'Breathing in, I know I am breathing in. Breathing out, I know I am breathing out.'

2. 'Breathing in a long breath or a short breath, I know whether it is a long breath or a short breath. Breathing out a long breath or a short breath, I know whether it is a long breath or a short breath.'

3. 'Breathing in, I am aware of my whole body. Breathing out, I am aware of my whole body.'

4. 'Breathing in, I calm my whole body. Breathing out, I calm my whole body.'

5. 'Breathing in, I experience joy. Breathing out, I experience joy.'

6. 'Breathing in, I experience happiness. Breathing out, I experience happiness.'

7. 'Breathing in, I am aware of the feeling [that is present now]. Breathing out, I am aware of the feeling [that is present now].'

8. 'Breathing in, I calm the feeling [that is present now]. Breathing out, I calm the feeling [that is present now].'

9. 'Breathing in, I am aware of the activity of mind [that is present now]. Breathing out, I am aware of the activity of mind [that is present now].'

10. 'Breathing in, I make the activity of my mind happy. Breathing out, I make the activity of my mind happy.'

11. 'Breathing in, I bring right concentration to bear on the activity of my mind. Breathing out, I bring right concentration to bear on the activity of my mind.'

12. 'Breathing in, I liberate the activity of my mind. Breathing out, I liberate the activity of my mind.'

13. 'Breathing in, I observe the impermanent nature of all dharmas. Breathing out, I observe the impermanent nature of all dharmas.'

14. 'Breathing in, I observe the letting go of all dharmas. Breathing out, I observe the letting go of all dharmas.'

15. 'Breathing in, I observe no craving with regard to all dharmas. Breathing out, I observe no craving with regard to all dharmas.'

16. 'Breathing in, I observe the nature of cessation of all dharmas. Breathing out, I observe the nature of cessation of all dharmas.'

"Bhiksus, that is the practice of conscious breathing, whose function it is to calm the body and mind, to bring about right mindfulness, looking deeply, and clear and single-minded perception so that the practitioner is in a position to realize all the Dharma doors that lead to the fruit of nirvana."

—*Samyukta Agama, Sutra No. 803 translated from the Chinese*

III

At that time, the Venerable Ananda was practicing meditation in a deserted place. It occurred to him, Can there be a way of practice if, when it is practiced to fruition, one will realize the ability to remain in the Four Establishments of Mindfulness, the Seven Factors of Awakening, and the two factors of wisdom and liberation? With this in mind, he left his sitting meditation and went to the place where the Buddha was staying, bowed his head and prostrated at the feet of the Buddha, withdrew a little, and sat down to one side. He said, "World-Honored One, I was practicing meditation on my own in a deserted place, when the question suddenly occurred to me, Can there be a way of practice if, when it is practiced to fruition, one will realize the ability to remain in the Four Establishments of Mindfulness, the Seven Factors of Awakening, and the two factors of wisdom and liberation?"

The Buddha instructed Ananda, "There is a way of practice which, if brought to fruition, will enable one to realize remaining in the Four Establishments of Mindfulness and, by remaining in the Four Establishments, the Seven Factors of Awakening will be realized. By realizing the Seven Factors of Awakening, wisdom and liberation will be realized. This way of practice is conscious breathing.

"How is conscious breathing to be practiced? A noble disciple practices as follows: 'Breathing in, I know I am breathing in. Breathing out, I know I am breathing out. Breathing in and breathing out, I know whether my in-breath and out-breath are short or long. Breathing in and breathing out, I am aware of my whole body.' While practicing like this, he dwells in the practice of observing body in the body, whether it be his own body or another body. At this point, the object of the bhiksu's observation that he follows closely is the body.

"A noble disciple practices as follows: 'Breathing in and out, I am aware of joy. Breathing in and out, I am aware of happiness. Breathing in and out, I am aware of the feeling [that is present]. Breathing in and out, I calm the feeling [that is present].' As he practices like this, he abides in the practice of observing feelings in the feelings, whether they be his own feelings or the feelings of another. At this point, the object of his observation that he follows is the feelings.

"A noble disciple practices looking deeply as follows: 'Breathing in and out, I am aware of the activity of mind [that is present]. Breathing in and out, I make the activity of mind happy. Breathing in and out, I bring concentration to bear on the activity of mind. Breathing in and out, I liberate the activity of mind.' As he does this, he abides in the practice of observing mental activities in mental activities, whether the mental activity is his own or that of someone else. At this point, the object of observation that he follows is mental activities.

"A noble disciple practices as follows: 'Breathing in and out, I observe the impermanent nature of things. Breathing in and out, I observe the nature of letting go. Breathing in and out, I observe the nature of no more craving. Breathing in and out, I observe the nature of cessation.' As he practices like this, he abides in the observation of phenomena in phenomena, whether they are phenomena in his own person or outside his own person. At this point, the object of his observation that he follows is phenomena.

"Ananda, the practice of conscious breathing to realize dwelling in the Four Establishments of Mindfulness is like that."

The Venerable Ananda asked, "World-Honored One, the practice of conscious breathing to realize dwelling in the Four Establishments of Mindfulness is as you have described. But how do we practice the Four Establishments of Mindfulness in order to realize the Seven Factors of Awakening?"

The Buddha said, "If a bhiksu is able to maintain mindfulness while he practices observation of the body in the body, if he is able to abide in right mindfulness and bind mindfulness to himself in such a way that it is not lost, then he is practicing the Factor of Awakening called right mindfulness. The factor of right mindfulness is the means that leads to success in the Factor of Awakening called investigation of dharmas. When the factor of investigation of dharmas is fully realized, it is the means that leads to success in the Factor of Awakening called energy. When the factor of energy is fully realized, it is the means that leads to success in the realization of the Factor of Awakening called joy, because it makes the mind joyful. When the factor of joy is fully realized, it is the means that leads to success in the realization of the Factor of Awakening called ease, because it makes the body and the mind light, peaceful, and happy. When the factor of ease is fully realized, the body and the mind are happy, and that helps us to be successful in the practice of the Factor of Awakening called concentration. When the factor of concentration is fully realized, craving is cut off, and that is the means that leads to success in the practice of the Factor of Awakening called equanimity. Thanks to the continued practice, the factor of equanimity will be realized fully [just as have been the other Factors of Awakening].

"When the noble disciple practices observation of the feelings in the feelings or observation of the activities of mind in the activities of mind or observation of phenomena in phenomena, he is also making it possible for the Seven Factors of Awakening to be fully realized in the same way as he does when he practices observation of the body in the body.

"Ananda, that is called the practice of the Four Establishments of Mindfulness with a view to full realization of the Seven Factors of Awakening."

The Venerable Ananda addressed the Buddha, "The World-Honored One has just taught the practice of the Four Establishments of Mindfulness that brings about the full realization of the Seven Factors of Awakening. But how do we practice the Seven Factors of Awakening in order to bring about the full realization of understanding and liberation? Lord, please teach us."

The Buddha taught Ananda, "When a bhiksu practices the Awakening Factor of mindfulness relying on putting aside, relying on no more craving, relying on cessation, he goes in the direction of equanimity, and then the strength of the Awakening Factor called mindfulness will help him realize fully the practices of clear understanding and liberation. When a bhiksu practices the other Factors of Awakening: investigation of dharmas, energy, joy, ease, concentration, and equanimity, relying on putting aside, relying on no more craving, relying on cessation and going in the direction of equanimity, the strength of these other Factors of Awakening will also help him to realize fully the practices of clear understanding and liberation. Ananda, we can call it becoming one of the different methods or the mutual nourishment of the different methods. These thirteen methods all advance when one of them advances. One of these methods can be the door through which we enter, and if we continue our journey after that using each of the other methods, we will arrive at the full development of all thirteen methods."

When the Buddha had finished speaking, Ananda was delighted to put the teachings into practice.

—Samyukta Agama Sutra No. 810 translated from the Chinese

Notes

[1] Savatthi (Sanskrit: Sravasti): The capital of the Kosala kingdom, about 75 miles west of Kapilavatthu (Sanskrit: Kapilavastu).

[2] *bhikkhu* (Sanskrit: *bhiksu*): monk.

[3] The *Pavarana* Ceremony was held at the end of each rainy-season retreat, the annual three-month retreat for Buddhist monks. During the ceremony each monk present invited the assembly to point out the weaknesses he exhibited during the retreat, in order to improve his practice and his character.

The full moon marked the end of the lunar month. Normally *Pavarana* was held at the end of the month of Assayuja (around October), but during the year in which this sutra was delivered, the Buddha extended the retreat to four months, and the ceremony was held at the end of the month of Kattika (around November).

[4] The full moon day of the retreat's fourth month (Kattika) was called *Komudi*, or White Lotus Day, so named because komudi is a species of white lotus which flowers in late autumn.

[5] field of merit: Supporting a good community, like planting seeds in fertile soil, is a good investment.

⁶ *Arahat* (Sanskrit: *Arhat*): The highest realization according to the early Buddhist traditions. *Arahat* means worthy of respect, deserving. An *arahat* is one who has rooted out all the causes of affliction and is no longer subject to the cycle of death and birth.

⁷ root of affliction (Sanskrit: *klesa*, Pali: *klesa*): The ropes that bind the mind, like greed, anger, ignorance, scorn, suspicion, and wrong views. It is the equivalent to *asava* (Pali): suffering, pain, the poisons of the mind, the causes that subject us to birth and death, like craving, wrong views, ignorance.

⁸ That is, the first five of the Ten Internal Formations (Sanskrit: *samyojana*): (1) caught in the wrong view of self, (2) hesitation, (3) caught in superstitious prohibitions and rituals, (4) craving, (5) hatred and anger, (6) desire for the worlds of form, (7) desire for the formless worlds, (8) pride, (9) agitation, and (10) ignorance. These are the knots that tie us and hold us prisoners in our worldly situation.

In the Mahayana, the Ten Internal Formations are listed in the following order: desire, hatred, ignorance, pride, hesitation, belief in a real self, extreme views, wrong views, perverted views, views advocating unnecessary prohibitions. The first five are called "dull," and the second five are called "sharp."

⁹ fruit of never returning (Pali: *Anagami-phala*): The fruit, or attainment, second only to the fruit of Arahathood. Those who realize the fruit of never returning do not return after this life to the cycle of birth and death.

¹⁰ fruit of returning once more (Pali: *Sakadagami-phala*): The fruit, or attainment, just below the fruit of never returning. Those who realize the fruit of returning once more will return to the cycle of birth and death just one more time.

¹¹ fruit of stream enterer (Pali: *Sotapatti-phala*): The fourth highest fruit, or attainment. Those who attain the fruit of stream enterer are considered to have entered the stream of awakened mind, which always flows into the ocean of emancipation.

¹² Four Establishments of Mindfulness (Pali: *Satipatthana*): (1) Awareness of the body in the body, (2) Awareness of the feelings in the feelings, (3) Awareness of the mind in the mind, (4) Awareness of the objects of the mind in the objects of the mind. For further explication, see Thich Nhat Hanh, *Transformation and Healing: The Sutra on the Four Establishments of Mindfulness* (Berkeley: Parallax Press, 1990).

¹³ Four Right Efforts (Pali: *Padhana*): (1) Not to allow any occasion for wrongdoing to arise, (2) Once it has arisen, to find a means to put an end to it, (3) To cause right action to arise when it has not already arisen, (4) To find ways to develop right action and make it lasting once it has arisen.

¹⁴ Four Bases of Success (*Iddhi-pada*): Four roads that lead to realizing a strong mind: diligence, energy, full awareness, and penetration.

¹⁵ Five Faculties (*Indriyana*): Five capacities, or abilities: (1) confidence, (2) energy, (3) meditative stability, (4) meditative concentration, and (5) true understanding.

[16] Five Powers (Pali: *Bala*): the same as the Five Faculties, but seen as strengths rather than abilities.

[17] Seven Factors of Awakening (*Bojjhanga*): (1) full attention, (2) investigating dharmas, (3) energy, (4) joy (see note 26), (5) ease, (6) concentration, (7) letting go. These are discussed in Section Four of the sutra.

[18] Noble Eightfold Path (*Atthangika-magga*): The right way of practicing, containing eight elements: (1) Right View, (2) Right Intention, (3) Right Speech, (4) Right Action, (5) Right Livelihood, (6) Right Effort on the Path, (7) Right Mindfulness, (8) Right Meditative Concentration.
The above practices, from the Four Establishments of Mindfulness through the Noble Eightfold Path total 37, and are called *bodhipakkhiya dhamma*, the Components of Awakening.

[19] Loving kindness, compassion, joy, and equanimity (Pali: *Brahma-vihara*): Four beautiful, precious states of mind that are not subject to any limitation, often called the Four Limitless Meditations. Loving kindness is to give joy. Compassion is to remove suffering. Joy is happiness that nourishes ourselves and others and does not lead to future suffering. Equanimity is relinquishing, with no calculation of gain or loss, no clinging to beliefs as the truth, and no anger or sorrow.

[20] Nine Contemplations: The practice of contemplation on the nine stages of disintegration of a corpse, from the time it swells up to the time it becomes dust.

[21] Joy and Happiness: The word *piti* is usually translated "joy," and the word *sukha* is usually translated "happiness."

The following example is often used to compare *piti* with *sukha*: Someone travelling in the desert who sees a stream of cool water experiences *piti* (joy), and on drinking the water experiences *sukha* (happiness).

²² *dharmas*: things, phenomena.

²³ Disappearance, or fading (Pali: *Viraga*): A fading of the color and taste of each dharma, and its gradual dissolution, and at the same time a fading and gradual dissolution of the color and taste of desire. *Raga* means a color, or dye; here it is also used to mean desire. *Viraga* is thus the fading both of color and of craving.

²⁴ Cessation, or emancipation, here means the ending of all notions, concepts, and wrong views as well as the suffering that is caused by these things.

²⁵ Letting go, or relinquishing, here means giving up any idea or any thing that we see to be illusory and empty of substance.

²⁶ "Joy" is the translation of *niramisa*. This is the great joy that is not to be found in the realm of sensual desire.

²⁷ Discriminating and comparing: That is to say, discriminating subject from object, comparing what is dear to us with what we dislike, what is gained with what is lost.

²⁸ Equanimity, or letting go (Pali: *Upekkha*, Sanskrit: *Upeksa*): Sometimes translated "indifference." The notion of giving up discriminating and comparing subject/object, like/dislike, gain/loss is fundamental. The Buddhism of the Mahayana school has fully developed this concept.

[29] *Sutta* (Sanskrit: *Sutra*): a discourse of the Buddha.

[30] Sutra 602 in the *Taisho Revised Tripitaka*.

[31] Parthia: Ancient country in Southwest Asia (northeast modern Iran).

[32] Sutra 125 in the *Taisho Revised Tripitaka*.

[33] Sutra 606 in the *Taisho Revised Tripitaka*.

[34] *Tsa A Han* or *Samyukta Agama* is Sutra-collection no. 99 in the *Taisho*.

[35] See Thich Nhat Hanh, *Transformation and Healing, Op. Cit.* (note 12, above).

[36] Thich Nhat Hanh, *Our Appointment with Life: The Buddha's Teaching on Living in the Present* (Berkeley: Parallax Press, 1990).

[37] Four Jhanas or Meditative States (Sanskrit: *Rupa Dhyana*, Pali: *Rupa Jhana*).

[38] Four Formless Concentrations (Sanskrit: *Arupa Dhyana*, Pali: *Arupa Jhana*).

[39] See Nhat Hanh, *Transformation and Healing, Op. Cit.* (note 12, above).

[40] The method of counting the breath has been widely accepted and has found its way into the sutras and commentaries. The *Ekottara Agama* (*Zeng Yi A Han*) (Sutra number 125 in the *Taisho Revised Tripitaka*, An Ban chapter, books 7 and 8) does not mention the technique of counting the breath, but it does mention the method of combining the

breathing with the Four Meditative States. Chapter 23 of the *Xiu Hang Dao Di* (Sutra number 606 in the *Taisho Revised Tripitaka*, book 5), called "The Breath Counting Chapter," identifies the method of full awareness of breathing with the method of counting the breaths. This sutra also refers to the Four Meditations.

[41] Sutra 606 in the *Taisho Revised Tripitaka*, chapter 23.

[42] Sutra 125 in the *Taisho Revised Tripitaka*.

[43] See note 23 above.

[44] See *Transformation and Healing*, note 12 above. See also *Our Appointment with Life*, note 36 above.

Parallax Press publishes books and tapes on Buddhism and related subjects for contemporary readers. We carry all books by Thich Nhat Hanh. For a copy of our free catalog, please write to:

Parallax Press
P. O. Box 7355
Berkeley, CA 94707